GOD'S MAN

GOD'S MAN

The Tales of a Reluctant Doctor

ALFRED SCHERER, MD

iUniverse, Inc.
Bloomington

God's Man
The Tales of a Reluctant Doctor

iUniverse books may be ordered through booksellers or by contacting:

iUniverse
1663 Liberty Drive
Bloomington, IN 47403
www.iuniverse.com
1-800-Authors (1-800-288-4677)

ISBN: 978-1-4759-6180-5 (sc)
ISBN: 978-1-4759-6181-2 (hc)
ISBN: 978-1-4759-6182-9 (ebk)

Library of Congress Control Number: 2012921355

Printed in the United States of America

iUniverse rev. date: 11/08/2012

CONTENTS

Chapter 1

God's Plan for a Life of Science

I am an old man. I practiced medicine for forty years and have been retired for ten years. During the last year of my practice, I was asked to see a particular patient. It was always my practice to do a standard exam of the patient and not neglect any procedure, starting at the head and examining from there. The first thing that I usually did was to examine the cranial nerves. In order to do this, I had the patient follow my finger with her eyes.

In this particular case, the patient could not follow my finger. There was a third nerve palsy, which affects the eye. This was very alarming.

The third nerve goes through a meningeal notch as it travels to the muscles of the eye. Pressure in the brain squeezes the nerve, causing palsy.

I immediately contacted a neurosurgeon, and the patient was taken to surgery, during which an epidural brain abscess was found.

The patient was young and had a family; the surgery saved her life. If that were the only success that I had ever had, it would have been worth my entire career. So now at age seventy-five, I look back and ask, was it worth it?

It all started in my youth. I was raised going to church. Very early, I realized that left to my own devices, I did things and thought things that were very bad. I was fortunate because a teacher in a children's meeting at church camp explained to me how I could handle my inner self. She told me, "People need their black heart changed. If you confess and repent, you will be forgiven and given the power to live properly."

I asked my mother all about this. My mother went to my teacher and said, "Alfred is spiritually hungry. Give him a chance to repent." I recognized that this was exactly what I needed. I put her solution into effect, and I met the lover of my being, who forgave me and enabled me to live my life with success.

You can listen to preachers, and they have a lot to say. The real truth is that success comes from confession, repentance, and forgiveness. I used to think that was easy, but over the years, I have found this is difficult for most people. My friends like to say that they sin all the time, and God forgives them. I never understood that. When I repented, I made an agreement that I would turn from my wicked ways and chart a new direction. The truth is that when God changed my heart, he gave me the power to resist sin. It always has seemed to me that I was bragging when I stated that I did not sin, so when confronted by my friends, I merely kept quiet. I never could understand their situation. When they repented, were they sincere when they agreed to change their ways? Why did they not use the power that a changed heart gave them?

I have always thought that I was forced to be a Christian. Basically, I had no other options. My life was very fragile; it hung on a thread. I was born without one small messenger from my hypothalamus called gonadotropin releasing hormone. This produced a lack of physical development. I was the smallest, weakest person in my age group. I know now what was (and is) wrong with me, but when I was a child, the doctors really had no clue.

They decided to give me a shot once a week of APL anterior pituitary like hormone, and I took series after series of these for the first seventeen years of my life. All it did was make me terrified of shots.

I basically ended up with three severe problems: I had asthma; I was small and slow to develop; and my urogenital tract was underdeveloped so I wet the bed. In my youth, I did not know my bedwetting was due to that lack of messenger from the hypothalamus. It made me feel very, very inferior. I prayed and prayed but never got any verbal answer until I was seventeen. My asthma was solved at the age of fourteen.

I seemed to make up for my lack in physical ability with my success in school. My mother taught me to read and write before I started kindergarten. She used to take me on her lap with a book, and we would read a page. Then she'd take a paper and tear a hole in it—this was the way she presented words on the page, and I would identify them. I did very well in school. I was fascinated with science and with chemistry, in particular. My scholarly success was not popular with my classmates. My verbal success did not do well for me, because verbal debate ended in physical violence. As a young person, I learned early in life that Gandhi was correct—an encounter that ends in physical violence harms the person who resorts to the violence more than the person he physically harms.

I was bullied. I was teased. The teasing did not bother me. I was quite articulate and could hold my own with anyone who wanted to take me on. This was not successful, however, as my peers just resorted to violence.

I had no answer to the violence.

In the process of being bullied, I was hit and physically thrown into a trimmed hedge. The high school principal's assessment was that I had asked for it. My mother's solution was that if I would bloody some noses, the bullying would stop. At twelve years old and in the seventh grade in the high school, I decided that neither the principal nor my mother was correct. I decided that I could decide for myself and realized that I had no help.

The bullies subjected me to violence until I burst out in uncontrollable crying. At the time, I thought this was a great defect, and I was totally ashamed that I broke down. I know now that it was a good thing and helped preserve my personality

I was born in Chicago. My father was transferred there because of the Depression. He migrated from Germany when he was twenty. My father had his heart changed in Germany, in a small Brethren church in Waldorf.

My father was the best Christian I have ever known. I have never known him to do anything wrong. He had built a house in Kansas City, and we returned there when I was seven years old. My parents put my brother and me in a Lutheran school in Kansas City, just a few blocks from where we lived. I went there my second and third grade years. There were only two of us in the second and later the third grade.

Dad believed that children should have responsibility. He thought they needed some livestock. We did not have cattle, but we did have goats. My mother thought that goat milk was superior to regular milk. We kept the goats in the building that later became the garage. Dad raised a garden. He would have probably planted fruit trees on the front lawn if Mom had let him. I hated the garden, only because I had allergies, and the gnats got in my eyes, and my eyes swelled shut. We lived a block south of Forty-Third

Street. Four blocks south of this was the border to the country. Five blocks west of our house was the border to the country. Dad farmed the vacant lot next to our house, and I was the prime weed puller. Later, Dad bought the lot and built another house for Mom. It was her dream house.

I took my wagon around the neighborhood and sold the excess produce from our garden. With the proceeds, I bought my first bicycle.

I was small, though, and could not reach the pedals very well. It took me forever to learn how to ride the bike. My son later just got on a bicycle and rode off. It took him about ten seconds to learn. In later years I discovered that my performance IQ was only 100, and it probably was the reason I had trouble learning to ride a bike. It also took me twenty hours to solo in an airplane. My friends sure kidded me about it.

When I was in the fourth grade, my parents took us out of the Lutheran school and placed us in the public schools. My brother was in the seventh grade and went to the high school. I attended the grade school.

It was right across the street from the medical school and five blocks from my home. It was quite a shock to go into a room full of students in the same grade, as there were only two in my grade in the Lutheran school.

From that time on, my brother and I were separated in our schooling.

When he entered the sophomore year in high school, he went to Central in McPherson, Kansas. That was a church school that had high school and junior college combined.

I then attended grade school in Kansas City. During one period, penmanship was taught. The third-grade teacher came into our room to conduct the class. She came to my desk and looked at my writing. I had learned how to write from my mother. In my writing, I closed the loop of the p, and I put points on the structure of the u. She had a fit. "That is not how you should write," she scolded me. "I am going to give you a failing grade." I cried all the way home. When I was in the first grade the teacher tried to teach me how to print. I was confused. I told her I did not write that way, and my mother did not write that way. She asked me how I wrote, so I showed her. She said that was fine, and there was no reason to learn to construct sticks and cookies to make printed letters. Later, when I told my mother that my teacher was going to fail me, she said. "Don't worry. It doesn't matter. Throughout your life, you will run into people who do not recognize that there is more than one way to do something.

4

If you learn to deal with the problem now, you will be way ahead of things." How right she was. My mother's motto was "Hitch your wagon to a star . . . and then get out and push it."

In the fifth grade, one of the class periods was for our science lesson.

A teacher came from another class to teach us. One period, she related the story of Antony van Leeuwenhoek, who built the first microscope.

She detailed what he saw in water and talked about seeing the corpuscles in blood. I was fascinated and entranced. I wanted a microscope, but my folks did not have the money to waste on my projects. My friend and classmate who lived across the alley got interested in microscopes, and his father bought one for him. It was more or less a toy, but it did work. Soon, he lost interest, and when that happened, I got hold of the scope. I went to the faucet and got a drop of water and looked through the microscope at it. I saw nothing. As hard as I tried, I saw nothing. I did the ultimate sacrifice and stuck myself and looked at a drop of blood. I saw pink stuff.

There were no corpuscles; in fact, there was no structure at all.

I was very unhappy. I went to the teacher. "Have you ever looked at water or blood?" I asked. When she said she had not, I told her, "I have.

You do not know what you're talking about. Water does not have creatures in it, and blood does not have structures in it."

She did not have a clue. If she had known, she could have told me that the city goes to great lengths to remove the beasties from the water that Leeuwenhoek saw and that blood has to be prepared in special way to show cells. It was much later that I found this out.

During this time of my youth, I learned something that I used all my life. My father told me that the use of alcohol and smoking was stupid. I seriously considered what he had to say. I decided that I did not need to alter my thinking with alcohol and that smoking invited fire and damage.

I agreed that it was stupid. I decided that there would be many times when I might do something stupid accidentally, so I did not have to do this purposefully. I used this principle throughout my life.

At the age of ten, I became interested in electricity and electronics.

I was told about the crystal set. It was the early radio that required no power supply. I discovered a rock in a rock garden that that had galena in it. I salvaged some of the crystals, and I used melted solder to make a pellet of solder that had a crystal of galena in it. My grandmother lived in Independence, Missouri. Her house was just east of the Mormon complex, and on Saturdays they had something like a flea market. It was called the campus. I found coils and headsets there, as well as many other parts. I only paid pennies for these. I constructed crystal sets from these parts. My neighbor, who was a sort of an electronics person, provided me with some field coils from very large motors. We put them in a bonfire and burned off the insulation. I uncoiled these and made a very large five-strand antenna. I put the antenna from the top window in our house out to the tree in the vacant lot. I will never know why it did not get struck by lightning. My crystal set was connected to that antenna, and I used the radiator in my room for a ground.

The main tower for radio station KMBC was only five blocks south of our house. I was told by a local ham operator that I would not be able to get any other stations. The signal from KMBC was so strong that you could almost receive programs from the fillings in your teeth. I worked hard, and at last I could bring in WDAF as well. I did it by using inductance and capacitance in parallel. Only much later in my education did I know the theory behind doing this.

I went to sleep listening to programs like Judy Canova and I Love a Mystery. I wore the headphones on my head so often that finally, they produced pressure sores on my ears.

At the age of twelve, I received a chemistry set. From that time forward I ate, breathed, and existed to learn chemistry. The small chemistry set later expanded into a laboratory of many chemicals and equipment in the corner of the basement. My father helped me, and we constructed a hood that I vented out the basement window. We constructed a centrifuge from a vacuum sweeper motor mounted in a five-gallon can. It routinely broke the glass tubes because it was so strong. When I went away to school, I gave all my equipment to the chemistry department of Central College, and some of the students used to kid me about how the centrifuge broke the tubes.

From the age of six to the age of fourteen, I suffered from very severe asthma. My friends called me Asthma Al. It was hardly a compliment. In the eighth grade, I missed half of the school days because of asthma. The school principal was very disturbed and wanted to dock my credits. The school graded on a number system, where one was equal to an A. I merely showed him my grades, which were mostly ones and only a few twos. He backed down and tried to work it out to help me attend more often. He did this by letting me report to the library, so that I could get the asthma under control and come to school later than the opening bell.

At the age of fourteen, I had one of my worst attacks of asthma. I could not get out of bed and became cyanotic. My mother called our new doctor—we'd lost our first doctor during the war. The new doctor came out and gave me a shot of adrenaline. This broke up the attack. He told my mother that he had a treatment for asthma, which was to take five hundred milligrams of vitamin C, four times a day. I started on that treatment, and the attacks quit as if I'd turned off a switch. I had been seen by doctors at the University of Kansas medical school; I was treated by the best. When I was in that school to become a doctor, I stopped the doctor who treated me as a boy and asked if he remembered me. He said he did.

I asked him what his reaction was to the fact that I no longer had any wheezing. He said my asthma would be back before I was twenty-nine.

He was wrong. I do not wheeze to this very day. I had prayed and prayed about this problem. This was an answer to prayer.

I had two high school teachers who befriended me. My biology teacher one day told me that a bright fellow like me should learn how to use a slide rule. He loaned me one with an instruction book and told me to take it and then come back and show him that I'd learned how to use it. I did not disappoint him. Another time, he took me to his storage area and told me to take samples of his chemicals so that I had the chemicals in my lab. I had a large camel-hair overcoat. The pockets opened into the lining of the coat.

I put those bottles in the lining of the coat and walked home, clinking all the way. I was so happy about this that it seemed my feet didn't touch the ground the entire way.

The other teacher who befriended me was George Hiatt. I owe a great deal to this man. He was my algebra teacher in my freshman year.

He also taught chemistry, although I never took chemistry from him. I spent hours after school, picking his brain for knowledge in chemistry.

I still remember how he taught me how to balance oxidation/reduction equations. When I was a sophomore, the local radio station in Kansas City had a radio show called It Pays to Be Smart. A group was chosen from a high school, and they competed with science questions. Mr. Hiatt asked me to take a qualifying test, and I was second best, so I was on the radio.

I did not win. I was asked what drug was used for malaria that turned the skin yellow. I had no idea. However, I surely owe a great deal to

Mr. Hiatt, my mentor. The answer to the question was Atabrine. I will remember that the rest of my life.

Mr. Hiatt's wife was the secretary to the dean of medicine at Kansas University. She watched my progress through medical school. I went to see Mr. Hiatt after I graduated from med school. I asked how he put up with my pestering him constantly over the years. He said I hadn't pestered him; maybe only once in a lifetime would a teacher have a student like me.

I developed an attitude for success in school. I learned very early in my schooling to have the attitude of I do not know "Teach me!" In later years, I gave a scholarship to a young man in my town who wants to be a doctor. I told him of this formula for success. He said that a teacher of chemistry had scolded him for not understanding some things in high school. He told the teacher, "You're right; I don't know. Teach me." He said it really turned the teacher on to hear him say that, and he was helped greatly.

In my sophomore year of high school, I took typing. During the last six weeks of the course, I had an accident with my bike, injuring my hand.

I was unable to finish typing or take the speed test. My teacher, Mrs. Alber, told me she would give me a half-credit and a grade of two. I spread my other grades out before her; they were mostly ones. I told her to give me a four minus and a full credit. She was astounded. I told her I took typing to be able to write papers on the typewriter, not to be someone's secretary. I needed the credit. She was so surprised that she granted me my request.

When I was in the fourth grade, the high school orchestra teacher came to my school and asked who wanted to learn to play the violin.

I raised my hand. This started a long path in music that I followed for my entire life. It has been very satisfying. I was always the best of the worst. My family did not have the money for private lessons, so I merely was taught at school. About half of the students in my class took private lessons. Even though I picked their brains as much as possible, they were always better than I was. However, I was always the best of those who did not take private lessons. I spent my life playing in orchestras as the first chair in the second violin section. Great Bend Community College had an orchestra that was formed by adults who practiced in the evening. It had several violins in each section. I joined and took my place at the end of the second violin section. As time went on, we lost and gained members, and I moved up until I was in the first chair. The person in the second chair noticed and asked why I had first chair. I said, "No reason. Do you want the first chair?" She said yes, and I gave it to her. The conductor then came in, noticed our changed positions, and promptly moved me back.

I can remember one good lesson I learned in orchestra when I was in high school. We had a rather corpulent girl who played the piano. One day I was sitting in one chair and had my feet up on another. She demanded that I take my feet off the chair. I responded, "It's not your chair." She hauled back and hit me and knocked me off of both chairs. A good lesson is not to snap back when you are not in your weight class.

We had a junior string class in the high school up to the eighth grade.

We had a recital at the end of eighth grade graduation. After the recital, the orchestra teacher said to me that a music professor from Kansas University had noticed me and suggested I make the violin my career. The problem was that I enjoyed playing mostly for myself. By the time I was satisfied with what I might play for others, the music no longer sang in my soul. I had to play it over and over to make it free from mistakes. Science was and still is the love of my life.

In high school, I was first chair in the second violin section. One day I guess I did something the conductor did not like. He sent me to last chair.

I then waited a period of time until things settled down and challenged the first chair. I won, and I was back to first chair.

Later, Mr. Brown, my orchestra teacher, went to Kansas University Medical School and became a doctor well before I did. He started practice in Stafford, Kansas. This was ten miles from St. John, where I practiced from 1975 to 1983. Before I left St. John, I took my violin to his office and played the Accolay Concerto for him. I think it really pleased him.

At the end of my sophomore year in high school, I transferred to Central Academy at McPherson Kansas. I took as many courses as was allowed and finished my last two years in one, graduating early from high school.

I thought that going to Central would be wonderful. I thought my fellow students would have the same goals and intent that I had, as it was a Christian college. I was completely wrong.

The students at Central knew what was right and knew how to do the right thing but did use god's power to keep sin from ruining their lives. They had a struggle with themselves and with everyone else. I would much rather be around a person who has no integrity than to be around a person who has integrity but cannot keep from ruining his life.

I now know many of those student that were my classmates at Central. For the most part they are fine upstanding people. All that shows it that God has a mighty way changing people's lives. They turned out to be great wonderful people.

The bullies existed at Central, just as they did at home, but there was one difference. I was taking a very large educational load by finishing two years' work within one year. In addition, I started off on the wrong footing. On my first night at Central, when I was 250 miles away from home in a strange room with a roommate, I got sick. I had never been sick like that before. I had abdominal pain and extreme vomiting. I spent the night running to the bathroom to vomit. I went down to the proctor's apartment and told him I was sick, but he did nothing that night. By the next morning, I decided to dress and try to get help. I was putting on my clothes when a tall man came into my room. He said he was Dr. Walters, and he took me to the hospital—I had appendicitis. The proctor in charge of the dorm had called him, even though the proctor thought I was just homesick. It was pretty scary for a sixteen-year-old to have surgery in 1948 with no family present. They used a spinal anesthetic, and I was terrified. They were not very good at it because they were careless and did not establish an anesthetic level before starting. When they put in the upper towel clips in the skin to hold the towels in place, I felt it and screamed.

When I was younger, I wet the bed, but over the years, I eventually controlled my bedwetting, probably just due to growing up. However, in the recovery period of the appendicitis, it came back. If there were any more ways to humiliate me, I can think of none. However, with time everything went back to normal. The only exception was that I still was bullied. I had a room on the second floor of the dorm with a roommate.

The proctor thought he would solve my problem by giving me a single room in the basement. All that proved was that he was unable to control things or be fair. During the year I was at Central, my mother was ill, and I called home frequently to find out how she was doing. I had to use the phone in the proctor's apartment. His wife made fun of me to the other students, telling them I was a momma's boy.

I had my first course in chemistry at Central, but my teacher had a limited knowledge of chemistry. She tried to explain the use of logarithms to solve chemistry problems. Back in my room after class, I tried her methods but it would not work. I asked a fellow student, Kenneth Shields, if he knew how to use logarithms. He said he did, and he showed me.

The next day, the teacher started in again to show us logarithms. I raised my hand and said, "That's not the way to do it."

"Would you like to show me how?" she asked.

I said I did, and I proceeded to explain the proper way. That did not make her happy.

Another time, she tried to demonstrate the method to determine the density of a metal. She handed out unknown samples of metals, and we put them in water, measured the displacement, and calculated the density.

We then were to give her the name of the unknown metal. One of the students had a sample of metal turnings. I recognized it as calcium. I was startled and started to say that I did not think he should put that in water, but I stopped because it was supposed to be unknown. "Go ahead and say what you think," the teacher said.

"That metal is calcium," I said, "and it will react vigorously with water."

"You go too much by appearances," she responded.

The student put the sample into a graduate and filled it with a measured amount of water. It went whoosh and hit the ceiling. The metal was calcium and we were lucky it did not explode. The teacher was not at all happy with me.

Margarete Palmer, my chemistry teacher, later went to Seattle and became a doctor. She then became a missionary to Africa for the church.

After I became a doctor, I had the privilege of sending her a lot of medical equipment In part, I think I made up for the angst I cause her at Central.

She had a favorite hymn that has followed me all my life. In part, it is:

> My gracious Lord, I own thy right
> to every service I can pay,
> And call it my supreme delight
> to hear thy dictates, and obey.
>
> What is my being but for thee,
> Its sure support its glorious end?
> Thy ever smiling face to see
> And serve the cause of such a friend.

I kept my bicycle at Central in the bike rack in front of the dorm, with a lock through the front wheel. Some of the students decided to try to ride it. In the process, they broke some of the spokes out of the front wheel so they could take it from the bike rack, but that made the bike useless. Then they decided to put the bicycle on the top landing of the third-floor fire escape on the back of the science hall. The president of the school came to me and asked what I was going to do about my bicycle.

I said, "I did not put it there. It can't be ridden anyway, so I don't care what anyone does with it." I presume he had it taken down, because it later appeared again in the bike rack. The important point, though, was that he did not care that I had a problem.

Later that year, someone turned on the fire hose outlet on the third floor of the science hall. It was on all night and ruined a lot of the building.

The library was on the first floor, and it was flooded, as was the basement, where there were stored potatoes that promptly decayed. The president cried in chapel over the incident. He was concerned with his problems but cared little for mine.

I knew of only one teacher who had any concern for me. Her name was Rose Anderson. I spent time talking with her. She taught me American history and civics, which were two required courses. She knew I was being bullied, and she gave me the best advice I ever had. She said, "You have a good mind, and when you go to college, none of your fellow students will act like they do at Central. No serious students resort to physical violence." How right she was. When I went to KU, there were about thirty students with interest in education just like me. We sat around and picked each other's brains. After Central, I never again was treated with physical violence.

At the end of my year at Central, the dorm proctor, Bob Wright, told me he expected to see me next year. I told him, "I have much to do.

I'm interested in an education and have no time for your or the school's nonsense. I have no intention of returning to this school." The best thing was that I took two years in one, which then launched me into my real education.

CHAPTER 2

How God Solved My Medical Problems

During the summer of 1949, I worked where my father worked. I had learned how to develop pictures during my time at Central. The wife of a teacher in the college taught a group of us after school. My father's company had a darkroom, and they desired to have an illustrated price list. This consisted of a seven-page fold-out of pictures of all the chair models that were made at Cramer Posture Chair Company. I used a speed graphic to take pictures and made contact prints of chairs. These then were pasted on boards to make a page that could be printed. A secretary used a varitype to produce the specifications that were under each chair. It took all summer for me to get all the pictures taken and put on seven boards for the fold-out. The fold-out was used for many years in the company. Since that time, I have always had a darkroom available, and I still have one in my present house.

When I got the job, they asked me to take a picture and show them the result. I used the enlarger and made the picture of a worker at a position.

I put the negative in the enlarger upside down, with the emulsion in the wrong position. That reversed left from right. Those I showed it to knew something was wrong but were unable to understand what it was, but they liked the picture. I remember that with humor to this day.

They wanted pictures that had no shadows or a line where the floor met the wall. That is not easy to do. I devised a system where I had a large roll of white paper that, when unrolled, could come down and let the chair sit on the end of the sheet, so that no line was present in the background. I then set the camera at a very small lens opening and had a person help me with floodlights. We more or less painted out each other's shadows with the moving light.

That was a good year, and it seemed I pleased Mr. Cramer. He knew I liked chemistry, and he came to me and asked me to research the process of bonderizing and parkerizing, which are treatments to prevent rusting. I did so, and they eventually set up what I recommended. In addition, I had several other suggestions, and they adopted all my suggestions.

One of my suggestions was to put a moving line place where the items were painted automatically and then went through a heated furnace continuously. It was put in place after I left. One of the other items I suggested was electrostatic painting.

Sometime later, one of my father's superiors wanted the expensive electrostatic system stopped. He blamed my father for using it, even though it was my idea. They had a confrontational meeting, and after a discussion, my father presented his position. He showed two chairs—one painted electrostatically and the other normally. He pointed out that the inferior one had half as much paint. The company fired the superior, and my father got his office.

When it came time for me to go to college, my brother, who was going to KU in Lawrence, Kansas, advised me not to go there for the first two years. He said that introductory courses and courses required for a degree were crowded and were taught by graduate students. He advised me to get all the simple stuff out of the way at a junior college. I applied and started school at Kansas City (Kansas) Junior College. I rode the bus to school each morning or sometimes a friend drove me there.

My brother wanted to go to medical school, and he took a course load that allowed him to go to college for only three years. This then made the first year in med school equal to the last year in college. I, however, thought I would do my work in chemistry. My brother persuaded me to take premed courses along with my desire for chemistry. He helped me set it up so I could get enough physics, chemistry, math, and biology to fulfill all possibilities.

With this in mind, I started my great adventure into real education.

The first thing I found out was that high school really was a waste of time.

Every course I took started at the beginning. I could have taken almost all the courses that I took and never gone to high school at all.

The junior college had a small orchestra, so I again was able to start up with my violin. This lasted for about half a semester. We practiced in an old barracks-like building called the annex. It was cold and drafty. The winters in Kansas City are quite cold. We met at seven in the morning, and the course only gave one hour credit. We only had three violins. The course was instructed by a local violinist from the Kansas City Orchestra, who was teaching for extra money. One morning, he stopped us and said to me that the music was terrible. I said, "It's really cold in here, and that makes it difficult to play."

"Get out!" he said.

"If I leave," I told him, "I'm not coming back."

"Get out!" he said again.

I went to the dean's office and told him I quit orchestra. "You' can't quit," the dean told me.

"Just watch me," I retorted.

"You'll get an F because it's too late to drop out," the dean said.

I knew that didn't make much difference and told him, "Just subtract that one grade point from one of my As."

At the beginning of the second year, the dean called me in and asked me to help in the orchestra. "I'm too busy with education to put up with that problem," I told him. He said, "I'll change your grade if you do," but I still refused. Then, at the end of the second year, when it was time to graduate, I was told I was to graduate cum laude—I hadn't expected this, as I thought I'd received an F, but I thought, If they don't know, I'm not going to tell them.

Later, when I went to KU, I was given my transcript as I enrolled in my classes. Under my grade for orchestra, a C had been pasted over the old grade. It seems the dean did not want that F grade on my record from his school.

In the years I was attending junior college, I again went back to our family doctor about my never-ending problem of weakness and lack of growth and strength. All he did was start me again on the series of weekly shots that I had taken since age five. I now was seventeen years old.

In junior college, I had my first course in beginning psychology.

During that time, I started on the great adventure into solving my physical problem. I was learning how to give myself shots without terror. I was required to write a paper in my psychology class, so I decided to write one relating to my fear of injections and just how I dealt with it. In addition, I described my struggle with my problem of being small and weak and how it felt to have some relief. I got an A on my paper and had many good remarks from my teacher.

One evening, my family went to the depot to get my brother.

On the way home, a very dramatic thing happened to me. I started shaking—something I had never experienced before and have never had happen since. It scared my parents, and they took me to the emergency room. The shaking was very violent. A doctor gave me a sedative, and the shaking stopped.

After that, a still small voice inside of me said that it was trying to get my attention. My reaction was that it certainly had my attention. I did a lot a praying in my first seventeen years but very few times had I ever had a direct answer. A year earlier, I had been praying, as usual, about my problems. It was obvious to me by this time that I would not have children.

One of the problems I faced was wondering who in the wide world would want to have me. I was kneeling beside a girl who was the daughter of one of my mother's friends. The still small voice said my mate had been chosen, and she was the person kneeling beside me. I chalked this up to wishful thinking. Now, the still small voice told me it wanted my attention. It instructed me to go to the endocrine clinic at the medical school.

This situation could not be wishful thinking, but I had no idea if this would work. I had never even thought of this. I went to my doctor who was giving me shots, and he said it was a good idea to go to the clinic.

When I got to there, Dr. Sirridge saw me and said that I had a real problem. He did a lot of tests, including one for bone age. My bone age was thirteen years old. He then said that more doctors were needed to have a look at me. I went to third floor, where five doctors stripped me and examined me.

After it was all over, Dr. Sirridge started a course of treatment. "I want to try the medicine you've taken all these years, only I want you to have one shot a day for two weeks. I understand you've considered becoming a doctor."

"That's right. I have," I answered.

He then said, "You can give your own shots. I'll show you how to do it."

He had no idea how terrorized I was of getting a shot. I certainly would not admit it to him. He then proceeded to show me what to do. He loaded the syringe and then plunged the needle into the top of my leg. He left it there while he finished telling me what to do. I was having a panic attack, but I do not think he ever found out. I went home, determined to conquer my fears. The first time I tried to give myself a shot, I drew the needle back, but at the last minute I chickened out—the needle that was used was an inch and one quarter long. I ended up bouncing the needle down my leg, putting red marks the length of my thigh. I finally learned to rest the needle on my skin and lunge it into my leg in one quick thrust. After two weeks, nothing had improved, and Dr. Sirridge decided to start me on the medicine that I have used my entire life it is testosterone. It is in the news about those who use performance-enhancing drugs. A person is supposed to have some of these products in his body. Athletes abuse things by adding more of this to their system. My problem was that I had no performance-enhancing steroids (testosterone) in my body. What I needed was what a person normally had. I have never wanted more than what was naturally needed. Under the direction of Dr. Sirridge, I had relief to my problem. I grew six inches in six months. My strength became normal, and I felt wonderful. It took some time, but I lost all my fear of shots,but I still did not know what was wrong.

With such a wonderful solution, I wondered about the other instruction of the still small voice. I decided to give it a try, so I wrote a letter to that girl I'd knelt beside in church. I bombed out; it produced nothing. I merely tried to start correspondence, but it did not occur. I now am seventy-five years old and have had many experiences with that voice, so now I know more about it, but then, I just chalked it up to wishful thinking.

I always worked in the summers. My father had a lot of contacts, and he got jobs for me. I always wanted to get my own job but never was able to. I worked a number of summers for the company where my father worked. When that happened, I went to work with him. Those times when we drove to work were good times for me, as I got to understand my father better.

I finished my second year in college in 1951. At that time, Zilpha Dickinson—the girl I'd knelt beside—finished her first year in college at Central. She needed to work to pay off her bill. My mother did not know I had written her, and she did not know about my experience with a still small voice. My mother offered to allow Zilpha to stay in a spare room and look for work in Kansas City. All of a sudden, things changed. Here she was, staying at the house where I grew up. I started getting to know her and took her places. One standard date every Saturday night was going to Youth for Christ in downtown Kansas City. We got quite serious and became a couple. We'd sit on the couch in the living room, enjoying each other's company. My brother likes long, complicated discussions on science, and he would sit down next to us and start in. We did not stop him, but it was not really what we wanted. I never said a word to him about it, but later, he was the one sitting with his girl on the couch. Only once did I reverse the situation on him, and he really exploded.

I told Zilpha that I could not have children. It did not seem to bother her; she knew we could adopt. I asked her to marry me, and she accepted.

In the fall of 1952, I enrolled in Kansas University. All my courses had been mapped out before my freshman year. All I had to do was to follow what I had planned. However, a person's plans have the habit of changing.

Very early in my youth, I repented, turned from sin in my life, and was given the power to live as I should. There was a problem, however, and it was that I did not get rid of the "want to" in my life. Preachers explained this and presented an answer. I was their best customer. Somehow, what they had to say did not work. I told God that whenever he was ready, I would be very happy to do what was necessary for the answer. Until this time, no answer came forth. However, in my junior year in college, I again heard the voice.

It said, "Gird yourself up because you are going to have to do something you do not want to do. The good things in your life can destroy you, just as sin can. You have to get rid of your ambitions and personal wishes. You cannot be a chemist." All those things I had rolled on my tongue and planned for had to be forsaken. Like Abraham, I had to deal with the Isaacs in my life. I was told I was to be a doctor. I argued, telling God I would not make a good one. "I will always be off balance," I said, "never knowing for sure that I have things right." He said he did not care, so I relented and changed my course. It was more or less up to the still small voice to see things through, but it was scary. Over the years, people have told me that I was not a very good doctor. My response to that was to look heavenward and say, "I told you so." And then God and I laugh and laugh.

The change did not alter my courses. I already had all the premed requirements, and I still stuck it out to take organic chemistry, physical chemistry, and calculus. I enjoyed every minute of these courses.

My brother set me up with a room in Lawrence. It was just three blocks south of the campus. My landlord was a wonderful man named Bruce Cameron. By luck, Kenneth Shields also was attending KU when I was there. He had a car, and he took me to church when I stayed in Lawrence. Most of the weekends, I went back to Kansas City to be with Zilpha.

During my senior year, I took physical chemistry. It was the most difficult course I had, and it also was the most enjoyable. I was well into the course, and I was scoring 65 on my tests. I went to Paul Gillis my teacher and said I was in trouble. I told him my score, and said, "This has never happened before. I need help."

He looked at his books and said, "You're making a solid B. Are you an undergraduate?" When I said I was, he said, "No undergraduate ever has made an A in that course." That calmed me down, and I ended with a B in the course.

During that first semester, the head office called for a number of us to come to the chemistry office. There were about ten. We were told that we were the cream of the crop and we were asked to be lab instructors for Chemistry 1. I said, "I don't want that job, but I would really like to instruct food analysis. I'm qualified." Dr. Brewster told me to talk to Professor Werner—he taught the course. Professor Werner said he really wanted me for the instructor. A week later, Dr. Brewster called me to his office. "I see you're premed," he said. "I'm not going to subsidize a premed student."

When I related this to Werner, he told me not to speak to Brewster again. "If you see him coming down the hall," Werner advised, "go the other way." Two weeks later, I was notified by Strong Hall The central office that I was hired, and one week after that, Werner had a heart attack and ended up in the hospital. He called me to say that because I knew his methods, he needed me to take care of the end of the semester with his other classes. In particular, he wanted me to supervise the students who needed to make up the final tests if they missed the regular time to take them.

The class in food analysis did not have a lecture; it only had lab.

Professor Werner died two weeks after the second semester started. I was left alone. I went to the chemistry office and told them I needed someone to supervise me, as I wanted to make sure my teaching didn't harm the students. They sent a teacher, and I showed him the entire course material.

He said that was very good—and I never saw him again. Later that year, my landlord told me that he'd met Brewster downtown, and he was really bragging on me. I had four students in a special junior/senior course. I had taken it the year before. When a student asked a question, I would say that the answer was in the book, and then I opened the book and showed him.

When I started at KU on the Lawrence campus, my parents rented an apartment in their house for sixty-five dollars a month. My brother had financial help from my parents, but he constantly had to ask for help. I told my parents I wanted a checking account and that if they could put sixty-five dollars a month in it, I would budget it, and that would be all I would need. It was not more than what my brother used, but he was not on a budget. We had quite an argument, but in the end, I won. I worked in the summers and applied that to school. On a monthly basis, it took twenty-five dollars for room, which left forty dollars for food and everything else. I ate in the student union cafeteria. If I ate macaroni and cheese for the main portion of the meal, I could eat for about a dollar a day. During the last semester at KU, I taught food analysis, and one of the students had a car. At the end of the day, we all loaded up in the car and went to Mom's down on Main Street. We got all we could eat for a dollar.

We starved all day and only ate one meal.

I kept account of the cost of my schooling. It cost $840 my junior year and $880 my senior year. With the money I made from instructing, it really cost very little. When I went to junior college, I lived in my parents' house, and it was really cheap.

Early in my schooling, I learned about mad money. I had a budget, but if I starved, and ate macaroni and cheese, and saved a dime here and a dime there, I could eventually have money that I could spend on something extra. Since that time, I have always had mad money. It never was a lot but just enough.

During my junior college years, my trigonometry teacher was Mrs.

Wenrich. She made us come into her office to get our grades. When I went into her office, she confronted me with the fact that I did not hand in the daily work. "I do not do your busy work," I told her. "I make A's on your tests."

"You cannot get an A if you do not hand in daily work," she insisted.

"What grade are you going to give me?" I asked.

"I'm giving you a B."

"I mastered trig—that was my goal," I informed her. "No one will ever care who I took the course from. I don't care if I receive a B."

I later found out I was not supposed to take trig and analytics in the same semester. No one told me this, so I did it. I was fortunate that in high school, the teachers respected my grades and did not care if I handed in daily work.

I had a wonderful teacher in analytics. I owe him a lot. About six weeks into the course, I went to talk to him. "I can do the work," I told him, "but I do not understand anything about the subject."

"You do not understand math," he responded. "There are only three numbers, and they have magnitude and direction. You only understand arithmetic. Arithmetic deals only with magnitude. Math deals with variables—a car does not travel at thirty miles an hour; it does so between limits." In about two hours, he turned my head completely around.

Modern math was supposed to address this problem on the lower grade level. I tried to work on this with my children but got nowhere.

During my senior year, I applied to medical school. I only applied to KU. After all, the medical school was only five blocks from the house where I grew up. My friends applied to a number of schools. The whole process was a sort of test. If I was to be a physician, then I should be able to depend on a higher power to see it come to pass. I was required to take a test before med school, and then I was scheduled to have an oral interview.

I was told that they were interviewing four hundred students for a class of one hundred medical students. They interviewed three of us at a time, and in my interview, most of the discussion was with the other two in the group. I was asked only two questions—why I wanted to be a doctor, and what my father did for a living. I do not even remember what I said.

However, I do remember a question they asked one of the others. They asked why they should take him and turn down the others applying for his position in the class. I do not think I could have answered that question if it had been posed to me.

After the interview, we were asked to go down to the dean's office. The dean asked if I wanted to know what I made on the entrance exam. "It makes no difference," I said. "I must have done okay, or I would not have come this far." He then asked me if I was the brother of Irvin Scherer. I told him yes, and he said he was through.

I did what I was supposed to do for medical school, but I did not try very hard because my heart was always in chemistry. I was accepted and was on my way to becoming a doctor; I have never been sorry. Like Paul before Agrippa, I could say that I was not disobedient to my heavenly vision. Although I no longer was in the process for a career in chemistry, God put some icing on the cake along the way. One such extra boost was my instructing the course of food analysis.

CHAPTER 3

MEDICAL SCHOOL WAS SCARY

My first year of medical school was on the Lawrence campus in 1953. I was still in a room at the Bruce Cameron house on South Illinois Street in Lawrence. Most of the medical students were in fraternities, but I never even gave it a thought. My brother was instrumental in starting a Christian fraternity. He was told that if he was not in a medical fraternity, he was not likely to succeed, because of the quiz files in the frat. However, he obtained an independent file to use when he started. I never had a file and really did not need one. I never had any trouble with grades in med school. At the end of the first year, I got a letter saying I was in the upper third of the class. By this time, Zilpha and I were very serious about each other, and we made plans to get married in the fall before my second year started. While I was in school at Lawrence, my weekends were back home in Kansas City as much as possible.

During the summer of 1954, I worked at Guston Bacon, which was a fiberglass plant. My aunt had a small house trailer she wanted to sell. I took Zilpha to it and asked if she would be willing to live in it, and if she was, I would fix it up. She agreed, and I bought it for seventy-five dollars.

That summer, I started tearing it down and fixing it up. I put a kitchen in one end and a bathroom in the other. One evening, I was having a very bad time. I had terrible hay fever, and my nose was running a river.

My father came out and asked how I was doing. I grabbed the end of the trailer and shook the entire unit. I almost cried. He looked at me and said he thought I was sick. He asked me to go in and said he would see what he could do. Several hours later, I went out, and Dad got up on

23

the end of the trailer and jumped up and down—it stood fast. I had a wonderful man for a father. We put a fold-down couch in the main part of the trailer, and that was the bed. The trailer was twenty feet long.

My boss at the fiberglass plant offered me insulation to use in my trailer. He gave me rolls of substandard material that I used liberally in the walls of the trailer. In December 1954, we pulled the completed trailer into a trailer camp two blocks below the school on Rainbow Boulevard.

We hooked up just in time before a snowstorm.

We lived in that trailer for four years, through the completion of my internship. I bought it for seventy-five dollars, put $425 dollars into it, lived in it for four years, and sold it to the first person who looked at it for four hundred dollars. After he bought it, I was sorry I had not asked more for it.

I had very little trouble in medical school. The first two years were basic medical science. Human anatomy was the big course in the first year. I was a chemist; I did not have any experience in medicine. My experience with doctors was not good, because I'd spent most of my youth in a doctor's office, waiting for hours to get a shot.

On the first day of school, we were divided into groups of four. We went down to the basement of Hayworth Hall and secured a body for anatomy. There was a large concrete tank filled with brown liquid. In that tank were floating bodies, and there was a block and tackle above the tank.

We took a noose on a pole and lassoed the body. We then hauled it up and put it on the concrete floor by a floor drain. Then we scrubbed the body with bowl brushes and placed in a box. Four of us carried the box up and then placed the body in the anatomy classroom in a small tank with liquid in the bottom. There was a tray that could raise the body up to table height, and a canvas cloth covered the body and kept it moist with preservative fluid. I had never seen a dead body, so this was a real shock to me. It did not take long into the year, however, before there was no problem at all.

I really enjoyed taking anatomy, but my dissection partner seemed to have a sensitive stomach. We took turns dissecting and reading the protocol. When working on the face and mouth, I got an inspiration.

The mouth was really gross. We were to pull a tooth, break the lower jaw, and follow the nerve through the mandible. I pulled the tooth—it was greenish-yellow. I said to my partner, "Put out your hand," and I put the tooth in his hand. He nearly lost his lunch.

At the beginning of the second year, I was married and living in the trailer in the trailer court north of medical school. The main course in the second year was pathology. It was still basic sciences, and as a student, I did not see patients. In the second year, however, I took a course called physical diagnosis, in which I learned to examine the patient. This was the start of a pattern that I would use for the rest of my career.

About halfway through the pathology course, my advisor, who also was a path teacher, told me that I was failing pathology. I could not believe it. I was making good grades on the tests, so I could not understand why she would tell me this. I told the assistant dean, Dr. Wilson, what I had been told. "If you were really failing pathology," he told me, "I would have been the first to know it. Who is your advisor?" When I told him, he said,

"Never see her again. Everything will be all right. You are not failing path."

That was the first of two times I was told I failed.

During the second year, med students were allowed to select an elective course. I chose the electron microscope. I spent six weeks learning how to use one. Because I'd taken photography, I was able to show the teacher how to make his picture come out much better. The electron microscope used glass plate negatives. These then were put in an enlarger and printed to a paper print. The print was mottled, because it was hard to make the microtome cut smoothly enough. I took the print and put it on a small upside-down tray in a larger tray. This left a small skim of developer on the print. I took a swab of sodium carbonate solution and used it to bring up the lighter areas of the print. This produced a better uniform picture.

The teacher was impressed and hired me to run his darkroom for him.

When the summer break came, I found out that Midwest Research Institute had an electron microscope. At that time, there were only three hundred in the country. I heard that they were not using it, so I wrote and told them I knew how to run it, and I wondered if they would be interested in hiring me. I got a call back. They did not have a project for the electron microscope, but my records showed I was an organic chemist, and they were very interested in hiring me. They asked me to immediately come out and visit with them at the institute because they wanted to hire me as an organic chemist. God put a little more icing on the cake.

Not only did I get to instruct a course at KU, but now I was able to start summer work as an organic chemist. This was the first job I ever got on my own. This was one better than my brother—he never got a job on his own before he became a doctor.

The first summer I worked at Midwest, we were doing a project for Lion Oil Company. It basically was making urea out of carbon monoxide and an amine. The amine we were using was aniline, and we made diphenylurea which made yield easy to determine. The reaction had many reactants and many variables. We subjected these to statistics and determined exactly what factors produced the maximum yield. In organic chemistry, yield is very important.

I was just a bench chemist. I did what I was told to do. Our PhD was named Lester. He was compulsive and very particular. He did not like me, and he made it well known. I paid little attention to this, however, and just did my job. The chemistry department had hoods which reactions were placed. These were vented to the outside On occasion, there would be a fire in a hood. There would be a loud whoop, and the chemists would grab fire extinguishers and run to put it out. I did not do so. They asked me why I did not help, and I said it was because I was only working for three months.

Lester decided to change the oxidizing agent in our reaction. The reaction was run in methanol as a solvent in a small oxygen tank, cold tested to 800 psi. It contained methanol and carbon monoxide at 100 psi and was heated to 100 degrees C. The other bench chemist was in the room reading data, and the thing blew up. It singed his shoes and deafened him, but it did not harm him. I maintained it was the oxidizing agent. I tried to get Lester to put holes through the wall, so the data could be read in another room. This was not done, but the reaction was put into the large pressure vessel and after it was opened, all there was in the vessel was carbon.

The work we did at Midwest quite often was used for patent. For this to happen, we kept a notebook, and at regular intervals, a knowledgeable person had to read, understand, and date what was done. I was asked to read and understand the work in the physical chemistry department. I was about finished when the other bench chemist asked me to help him break down the large pressure vessel. I went into the bomb room and started to unbolt the vessel. I looked up at the gauge on the top of the chamber, and it was completely over and on the peg. That scared me. It meant the reaction had exploded and the container might just do that also. They said I turned white. I pulled out all the plugs, ran out of the room, and closed the door. They were all there, watching me and laughing. It seems they took the needle off the center pivot and put it over on the peg, reporting above 25,000 pounds. The head of the department saw this and asked if they really were putting it to that high of a pressure.

The job I had at Midwest was the only job I had that I was eager for the weekend to be over so I could continue what I had to do. I no longer had a career as a chemist, but God gave me that time to enjoy because he enjoyed seeing me happy.

Lester could not stand to see anything out of place. In organic chemistry, we had the best chemical hoods because we were organic chemists and doing reactions on the bench without a hood was dangerous.

The physical chemistry section wanted to use some hoods, so they came to Lester and asked him if they could use them. He said yes. They were making borane compounds. Some of them caught fire on exposure to air.

When they did, they left very fine boric acid on every surface exposed to the process. This is what happened to the hoods. The physical chemistry section left our hoods in that condition. Lester was very unhappy. He went to Dr. Goodwin, the head of the section, and complained. He stated that if that happened again, he would quit.

I recognized that I probably would not be hired in summer of 1956, because it was obvious that Lester did not like me. Still, I called Midwest at the beginning of my summer vacation of 1956—the worst they could do was say no. To my surprise, they told me to start work immediately.

When I arrived, one of the chemists, a guy named Fred, asked me if I noticed anything different. He said that there had been a fire in the hood, and they had to repaint the room.

"What happened to Lester?" I asked.

"Do you remember the incident with the boric acid in the hoods?" Fred responded. "Lester made a fuss again. When he did, he was told that at Midwest, we work with each other, and if he could not do that, he needed to leave. He didn't want to lose face, so he left."

The organic chemistry department wanted to publish their method of statistically determining yield from the project from Lion Oil. They were not allowed to do so, as the work was for patent. They had a project for making a product that would not freeze at 32 degrees and would not decompose at 700 degrees. They thought they could do this with an asymmetrical urea. In order to do so, they needed amines. They felt they could make these amines that had not been made before, and do it with the process they wanted to publish. It required reductive alkylation.

Originally, we were using lithium aluminum hydride in ether. I ran one or two reactions with this, but it was very dangerous. I had a liter of ether with the hydride in it and if opened to air, it would catch fire.

We settled on the Leuckart reaction, which produced three amines, and the various yields were determined and a statistical method determined exactly which variables would produce the most yield of each one.

The process took the entire summer, and I finished just in time. I asked if my name could be on the paper, and they allowed this to happen.

I am most proud of what I did in just those three months. I had total enjoyment.

When I started medical school, I learned that the licensure law was about to change. It did so one month after I graduated. I decided I needed to get a better certification so I applied to take national boards. This was a test that required two days of testing after the second and fourth years in medical school and an oral exam after internship.

The third year in medical school was the start of clinical medicine. My first rotation was in surgery. This also was completely new to me. I was on the service of the head of the department. I was present at his surgeries.

The surgical area was a rectangle open to surgery, with drapes enclosing the rectangle. The surgeon would then point, and the student was to tell him the anatomy. It was fortunate that I was very good in anatomy. I think I made an impression on Dr. Albritton.

We had two sections in surgery. The first was at the medical school, and the second was at the VA hospital. Final exams were after my last day at the VA hospital. It snowed a large amount the day before the finals. I was to go to the VA that morning, but I did not go because I had finished my work, and I felt it would be hard to go through the stress of traveling in the snow and then take finals.

A classmate in surgery came to me and said that Dr. Higgins had stated that the only one who'd failed surgery was the one who did not show up that morning. This was the second time I was told I was failing. I went to Dr. Albritton's office and told him my problem. "You're not failing," he said. "Do you know what you made on the finals?" When I said no, he told me I made the highest score of the class. This seemed very good, but in reality, the reason I scored so high was because I had taken the national board exams. I knew how they worked, and I knew that the last part of the test took a good deal of time, so I rushed though the true-or-false and multiple choice parts and was able to finish. I am sure my classmates did not know what they faced and did not finish. Our grades were superior, satisfactory, or unsatisfactory. I got a superior in surgery.

The internal medicine section was divided into two parts. I spent the first part at the medical school and the second part at Menorrah Hospital.

The section at the medical school was for Dr. Delp and Dr. Weber. Dr. Delp was the best, and it was a great honor to be on his service. However, he was very difficult.

I had a patient who was very sick. I did not understand why he was put at the far end of the hall, a long way from the nursing station. I was worried about him. I had to write a paper anyway, so that evening, I pulled up a table and sat in the hall outside his room, writing the paper.

I could look into the room and watch the patient. Later that evening, he became short of breath and went into pulmonary edema. I ran to the nursing station and alerted the nurse. In a very short time, the residents came and started to work on the patient. To my surprise, Dr. Delp came, and they took a pint of blood from the patient, and he recovered. After things settled down, Dr. Delp looked at me and asked me what I was doing. I said, "I had to write the paper so I thought I might as well do it in the hall."

It was common for Dr. Delp to quiz the six of us in our student group constantly. One time in the hall, he said that the patient had an elevated TPK and asked me what that meant. I told him that it generally became high in biliary obstruction. He then went around the group, and they all disagreed with me. That did not encourage me. He then said, "Boys, boys, boys," and headed for the treatment room to discuss it. I thought I was going to really get reprimanded. However, it turned out I was correct, but Dr. Delp never gave me any credit.

Another time the resident came to me and asked me what I thought about a certain patient. This patient had a chief complaint that the elastic in his stockings made marks on his legs. I told the resident that as far as I could tell, he had no medical problems. The resident said, "Dr. Delp thinks the patient has aortic stenosis."

"How could that be when has no murmur?" I asked. "We should prove he does not have it." So we ran a great number of tests, ending in using the fluroscope to show he had no calcification.

Our group was in the hall, and Dr. Delp asked me what I thought about the patient. I told him that as far as I could tell, nothing was wrong.

He just shook his head, and off we headed to the treatment room. He then asked if I thought the patient had aortic stenosis. I then spouted off all the tests we'd done to prove he did not have it, and I gave the normal results. This really surprised him. He stopped for a moment. He then said, "Scherer, if you saw the sun rise in the south, what would be wrong"?

I said, "My observations, Dr. Delp." Nothing more was said. As far as I know, the patient did not have aortic stenosis.

Dr. Delp was a showman. He had a session called a clinical pathological conference that was held at noon on Saturday. He did this to show that he could get the entire medical school class to show up at lunchtime on a weekend and hold them spellbound. The entire class came to the third floor auditorium to see a group of six seniors perform for Dr. Delp. The group of six seniors sat in six designated seats in the auditorium. They then presented and discussed a case that they had been given the Wednesday of the week before. The discussion was divided into a differential diagnosis, the EKG, and the X-rays, leaving three students left to be called upon.

The differential was the important part. We were given a summary of the case on Wednesday, and we spent a good deal of time in the library, working on the differential diagnosis. The differential was presented first, and the person assigned to the task stood before the entire class of three hundred and listed every condition to consider, told why each one was not the diagnosis, and then why the final diagnosis was decided. This summary was then placed on a 3 x 5 card to use in the presentation.

One member of our group did not show up in the library until an hour before we were to present. He then came to me and asked,

"Will you give me your card if I'm chosen for the differential?" I told him I would and that I would coach him on it. I agreed to this because if one man did badly, we all suffered. Well, I was chosen for the differential, and Our wayward member was given the EKG. Dr. Delp then told our group to ask him some questions. We did, and to some he would say he wanted that asked in the meeting. He played the session like a fine violin. The member given the EKG asked me what he should say. Since I had the differential, I ran our group. I told him the EKG was normal for a child and that he should say just that and sit down.

The one who gives the differential sits in the seat on the end of the row. Later, after things changed, the seat was removed, and the last time I saw it, the library had it preserved as an exhibit.

I have always thought that when I gave that differential, it was the worst ten minutes in my medical training. I got up before those three hundred students and gave the differential. I was in shock, and I stood there too long. Delp had to tell me to sit down. He then asked for the discussion of the EKG. The student got up and said exactly what I told him to. When he started to sit down, Dr. Delp said, "Wait a minute. How does the child's EKG differ from that of an adult?"

He stood there for a time, and finally he said, "I do not know."

All of a sudden, Dr. Delp was asking me about the EKG. So now I was to tell him. Lucky for me I could tell him. He did not say if it was right or wrong. He just went down the row, asking each one if he agreed. They all shook their heads yes, and it was over.

A new idea was put forth on the internal medicine service—it was decided to take a pathologist along on rounds. This resulted in a real discussion of the pathology of the problems we saw. In one case, the patient had kidney disease, and there was a discussion as to just exactly what was going wrong. The attending physician and the pathologist disagreed. If the pathologist was correct, there would be refractile bodies in the urine.

I was asked to prepare a urine sample for the pathologist to demonstrate.

I took about a gallon of the urine and centrifuged it in one-half ounce tubes to prepare a concentrate. I then took it to the pathologist. The next day, he came with pictures and demonstrated refractile bodies. I still do not know if I screwed up the result by centrifuging so much urine. I never told anyone of my procedure.

When it came time for my obstetric rotation, I was set up for service at Kansas City General Hospital. That was across town. I found out that there was one place still open at the medical school. If I could get that, I only had three blocks to walk. I went to the dean's office and talked to the assistant dean. He was not impressed, but the dean asked to see me. When I met with the dean, he asked me, "Do you like boxing?"

"No," I said.

"I need a student to give services at the Golden Glove boxing in the municipal building downtown."

"I'll go," I said. All I learned was that I knew nothing about injuries in boxing, but I enjoyed seeing how it was done. After that, I was informed that I would be assigned to the obstetrical service at the medical school.

I decided I had to have a car. I had no money to speak of. Zilpha and I lived in that small trailer. Zilpha taught school; I worked in the summer.

Between both of us, we never had to ask my folks for help. We even had little extra, but I decided to ask for a loan. My parents banked at the Twin City State Bank. Growing up, I took my father's check to the bank every Saturday. The teller watched me grow up. Now I was in medical school, and he was president of the bank. I asked him for a loan, but he said no. I still do not understand why he turned me down—he knew me. I went to the medical school and asked if they had money I could borrow. They did, and I borrowed nine hundred dollars to buy a car. After I started to make money in my internship, I paid them back.

The school had a section of time set up to farm us out to a local doctor and then a state school. I was sent to Dr. James Marchbanks in Oakley, Kansas, and I spent time at Parsons State School.

I was a lucky person to spend my time with James Marchbanks. He was a wonderful doctor. I have always tried to be much like him. After I was there for some time, I made the mistake of commenting to someone that Dr. Marchbanks was five years behind the times. He and I were drinking coffee one day, and a nurse who'd heard my comment asked him if he knew what I'd said. When he said no, she told him. I wanted to curl up and hide. Dr. Marchbanks sat there a minute . . . and then he said, "That's about right." I could have hugged him. He was a very secure person. It would be nice if I were as secure.

At times, Dr. Marchbanks left to be with Explorer Scouts. When he did, I was left with his partner, Dr. Oney. One time, Dr. Oney took care of patient who was eight months' pregnant and having gastric bleeding.

He asked me what I would do. I said I would treat the ulcer, and if I could get it to stop, I would wait to deliver the baby and then see if the ulcer needed surgery. "You're wrong," Dr. Oney said. "We're going to do a gastrectomy and C-section." That seemed to be a bit much, but I made no argument. He called Dr. Reynolds from Hays and scheduled surgery. Dr. Oney criticized me constantly, even through the entire surgery, but when he was sewing up the very large incision, I snapped. He'd said, "If the patient complains of discomfort after that long incision, I sure will know what is wrong." Then I said, "That would be the first correct abdominal diagnosis you've made since I've been here." The air turned blue, and he swore and called me a vile names. The surgeon had listened to Dr. Oney the entire time, and I could see he was laughing behind his mask.

Then Dr. Marchbanks came back. He called me into his office and said, "I hear you had a problem with Dr. Oney."

"I guess so," I said.

"If you have any more trouble with him," Dr. Marchbanks told me, "remind him of the bladder cyst."

It seems on a surgery, Dr. Oney had explored the abdomen, only to find a round mass in the pelvis. He explored further, and he found what he thought was a cyst in the bladder. So he opened the bladder, only to find a Foley catheter, with the balloon filled with water. He forgot the patient had a catheter in the bladder. Dr. Marchbanks told me to tease him about that.

Near the end of medical school, we were to decide on internship. Some of us found out that Bethany Hospital needed its internship filled. We got together a group of seven seniors and went to negotiate the internship.

The idea was to persuade the doctors who attend patients at the hospital to give us hands-on teaching. That was the agreement, and for the most part, they did.

It was a rotating internship. We were allowed an elective six-week period. There was a wonderful person working at the hospital in order to get things worked out for practice. His name was Archie Tetzlauf, and he had a residency in anesthesia. I wanted to learn anesthesia, and he taught me in those six weeks.

I think anesthesia is very hard to learn. I had a very hard time learning just the depth of anesthesia. Archie used to say that there are only three levels: too light, too deep, and just right.

One procedure every intern wanted to master was tonsillectomy, and I was giving anesthetics. The child was put to sleep with ether vapor, which was poured into his mouth through a tube from a vaporizer. I was wearing a headlight and could direct the light by moving my head. I would shine the light so that the attending could see, but I made it difficult for him to take the surgery away from the intern. When I gave the anesthetic, the intern actually got hands-on instruction.

One day I was on a surgeon's service and a patient came in complaining of a spiking fever and the flu. I examined her, and she had an extremely harsh systolic murmur. I called Dr. Heiser and told him I thought she had a bacterial infection of her heart valve subacute bacterial endocarditis (SBE), and I wanted to stop the broad-spectrum antibiotic and do blood cultures.

He said he would have a cardiologist look at her.

Some time later, the cardiologist came to the emergency room where I was working and asked for the intern who thought a patient had SBE.

I said I was the one. He said the patient did not have blood in her urine, and he then proceeded to make fun of me and my diagnosis. The truth was that Harrison's Principles of Internal Medicine said that if a patient had a spiking fever and a harsh murmur, that patient had SBE until proven otherwise. The line was written in the textbook in italics to emphasize the point. I went to the chart and wrote that this was the case—a spiking fever an harsh murmur—but that no one was doing anything, and the patient would die. I went to the pathologist and told him my story. I said, "Unless someone does something very aggressive, you will be doing the postmortem, and you will see vegetations on the valves."

During my internal medicine tenure I had read most of Harrison's textbook, and I could leaf thought the pages and find the quotation on the page.

I lost track of the patient, but one night, weeks later, I was called to the third floor, and there, under an oxygen tent, was the patient. She was dying. I told the nurse. "This patient probably has SBE." The nurse said, "Yes, Dr. Ledger has seen her, and he concluded that she has SBE."

The patient died, and I pronounced her dead. I talked to the family and asked for a post, and they agreed. The next day I went with the pathology assistant to the funeral home, got the material for the postmortem, and spent time observing it being done. She had infections on her valves.

I have always looked very much younger that I am. For this reason, I have not been taken seriously a good deal of the time. While I was an intern, one of my wife's relatives was a nursing student. Much later, she said that she overheard a doctor making light of my abilities, only to be corrected by another who said I was the best diagnostician that the hospital had. The only reason anyone might have said that I was the best diagnostician was because of my diagnosis of the case of SBE.

I made friends with the pharmacist at the hospital and often talked with him and learned from him. I was in the pharmacy when a Dr. Kennedy came in asking for sodium glutamate—he said he had a patient who needed it. "I have a doctor who is bleeding from esophageal veins and is in hepatic coma," he explained.

"You don't need glutamate," I informed him. "You need argenine, but that's an experimental drug and not available in the pharmacy. I know Dr. Brown at the medical school, however, and he's using it. I could call him." Dr. Kennedy asked me to do so. I went to the medical school, and Dr. Brown gave me instructions. He said that I had to put down a tube and flush all the blood out of the gut, or it would not work. So I took it back, and Dr. Kennedy asked me to help. The ill doctor was in an oxygen tent and unresponsive. I got up on the bed to put the tube down his throat—this was very difficult because the patient could not swallow. I had to put my finger down to control where the tube slid. That was just the time, however, that the patient decided to die. That is something I will remember until I die. The doctor-patient's office nurse had been giving him private duty care, and all she could say was that I killed him. That was very disturbing, and I will never forget it. Of course, I had nothing to do with his dying; I was trying to save his life. Patients quite often die when they have hepatic coma.

The doctor who prevented my life from being destroyed was named Sirridge. His wife (also called Dr. Sirridge) was a hematologist. She was a wonderful teacher, and I owe her a lot. I watched her doing bone marrow biopsies using the sternum. I asked her to teach me, and she did. I have used her training, over and over again, during my career. One day, she said that the worst sore throat a person can have is probably infectious mononucleosis. One night, I saw a nurse from the hospital in the emergency room. She had egg-sized nodes in her neck. I told her she had "the kissing disease" (mononucleosis) and laughed and ordered a test for it. Of course, mononucleosis is not caused by kissing. Some time later, I had some enlarged nodes and a terrible sore throat. I put up with it for a while, but then I saw Dr. Sirridge, the hematologist, in the lab. I reminded her that she'd said the worst sore throat was mono and said I must have mono. She ran a heterophile, and it was positive, so I was stuck with being ill. I did not give in to it, but I went to my friend in the pharmacy and asked if he had anything that might help my sore throat. He gave me an old remedy of iodine in glycerine, and I used it as a throat swab; it really helped. From that time on, in my practice I used that remedy for sore throats very effectively.

On the day I finished my internship I got a notice in the mail that my draft status was 1A. My brother had received help from the government and paid back two years for every year of help by enlisting in the navy for two years for every year of help. I applied early in my medical school years for assistance but was turned down. After receiving my draft notice, I called the draft board and told them I would gladly join the army as a doctor. They told me that I had to have a physical, but I would have to wait my turn. What was I to do?

CHAPTER 4

AN ADVENTURE-OF-A-LIFETIME PRACTICE

I now was faced with the problem of what to do—I could hardly start a practice until my draft status was settled, and that could not happen until I had an induction physical.

A wonderful doctor in Wichita, Milton Lindley, found out about my problem and offered to let me practice in his office until my status was settled. Dr. Lindley attended my church, and I had known him for a long time. His offer worked out great for me. He was very kind to me.

So it was off to Wichita. Zilpha quit teaching school, and we rented an apartment. I settled in, and Milton asked me if I could give anesthesia. It seems Milton also had given anesthesia and he wondered if I could also. I told him I was trained at Bethany, and he told me to talk to Dr. Tinterow.

When I did, Dr. Tinterow asked me if I could give anesthesia and I said I could. He sat me down to manage a case at Wesley Hospital. After a time, he was satisfied, and he asked me to run his program at Wesley. He had four nurse anesthetists and did about three cases every morning. I was to start every case and have a nurse to circulate. I sat and drank coffee, and if there was a problem, I went and solved it. If there was an unusual case, I was to do the case. In the afternoons, I had a practice in the office, and in the evenings, I made rounds on the cases we were to do in the following day. We were rather busy.

Dr. Tinterow was a wonderful teacher. The regular procedure for tonsils was to blow ether vapor into the mouth after inducing with Vinethene.

This has limitation to about twelve years of age, because you generally cannot get enough ether into a patient that big by insufflation. However,

I watched Dr. Tinterow do a thirteen-year-old patient. I told him if he could do it, I could. So I decided to do just that on a twelve-year-old.

My patient, however, started to lighten and wake up in the middle of the procedure. What was I to do? Cyclopropane is very potent and quite compatible with ether, so I cracked the valve to cyclo and smoothed out the anesthetic. However, it is potent enough to affect anyone, and when Dr. Price stuck his head down to see better, he came up complaining that he did not know why he was getting dizzy. It all worked out fine, and I never told him what I did.

Dr. Tinterow was into many things. He would put staples in people's ears to help them lose weight, and he got deeply involved in hypnosis.

I think he really liked me, because he took me with him to some of his learning sessions for hypnosis. It really helped me. I learned a technique called "waking suggestion," and I used this procedure during my entire career. I had been terrified of shots when I was a kid, and I vowed that would never happen to the patients in my practice. The course taught never to use shocking words like shot, cut, or hurt. From that time on, I never gave "shots"; I gave "mosquito bites." I'd say to the child, "Have you ever been bitten by a mosquito?" While the child was thinking, I'd give the injection. I also never used the word "cut," and I would use the word "bother," not "hurt." I learned how to control a child's thinking through a conversation that controlled his or her thoughts. In the emergency room, I would talk about pets. Then I would say, "Do you know what I have as a pet? I have a kangaroo." The child then would have to think of those words. I learned to let the child have control by telling him to let me know if something bothered him very much. I would say, "I will stop for a while if it bothers you," and this would give the child a portion of control.

I only rarely called Dr. Tinterow to help. I had a case of 85 percent body burn for skin graft. I called Dr. Tinterow and told him I thought I could not do it, because the patient was too sick for me to handle. He came and managed the case. He gave a muscle relaxant and tried to put a tube in. He was unable to do so, and he asked me to try. I looked, and everything was burned. I could make out no landmarks. The patient got almost black, and my heart was racing, when all of a sudden he took a breath. The relaxant had worn off. The surgeon then did a tracheotomy, and we put a tube in there.

I asked him for help with a patient who weighed over five hundred pounds and needed a rectal abscess incised. I told Dr. Tinterow I did not think I could raise the chest with respiration. When we tried to move the patient to the operating table, the gurney started to collapse, so the surgeon just incised the area on the gurney without an anesthetic.

One time I was giving an anesthetic to a patient with a large burn and a temperature of 103 degrees. I was not told they were going to bring in a motorized dermatome which was an explosive hazard. I said nothing, but the surgical supervisor came and asked me what anesthetic I was using. "A good one," I told her.

"Is it explosive?" she asked.

"Yes."

"Change it," she ordered.

"No," I responded. "I cannot give enough oxygen with the other anesthetics to be safe."

Tinterow happened to be in the building, and soon he came and asked me what I was using. I told him cyclopropane. He said change, and then I told him to set down. I went to the lounge and drank coffee. When I came back some time later, I could see what he was using, but I asked, "What are you using, doctor?"

"Shut up," he snapped at me. Of course, I knew he was using cyclopropane; I could see it.

We depended on the surgeons to give us business. A wonderful doctor named Van Parmalee, who gave anesthesia, would say, "Every day is Christmas, and every surgeon is Santa Claus." The anesthesia machines have a system called a circle. It has two mushroom valves on the top.

If you put the mask to your face and take a breath, you can check the valves by how they respond to breathing. Most of us used this method. Of course, you put oxygen in the bag to do this. Van did this but somehow, he had a leaky cyclopropane valve and had cyclo in the bag. He took only one breath and ended up on the floor and had to have stitches in his head.

We never let him live it down.

I never had an anesthetic death, although they do occur. Sometimes, the doctor does not even know what happened. That happened to another group while I was at Wesley. When such a thing happens, everyone who can goes in and helps. I did my best, along with others, to help when a six-year-old patient for plastic surgery died. Later, Dr. Tinterow said there was only one good thing about that. I said, "I know of nothing good about it." He said, "Oh yes—it did not happen to our group."

I gave quite a few spinal anesthetics. We did a lot of talking in the doctor's lounge, and one of the groups only had two anesthetists. I must admit they were pretty good, but one of them told me that he never failed when doing a spinal tap on a patient. I must confess that I have failed at times, and I have had bloody taps. The doors to surgery have two windows, one in each door. As I was walking past and looking in, I saw this doctor, and he was having trouble with a spinal. I watched, and he never got in.

Then he looked up and saw me. I never said a thing, but he would never talk to me again.

Nine months went by, and then I was given notice to have an induction physical. They gave me a physical with the general run of inductees. I had heard that army physicals are not complete, but this is not so. They did not know I was a doctor, but I knew what they were doing, and they did a very good job. I gave a written history of my medical problems. I have always been dependent on periodic shots and had a lengthy history. After the physical, I received a letter, with a form to be filled out by an internist.

I was asked to see the internist for another physical. After I sent that in, I received a letter notifying me that I was classified 4F.

I decided to look for a place to settle and practice. I talked with Dr. Tinterow. He told me he was very pleased with my work, and then he added, "We only lost one surgeon when you were working for me."

"I know," I said, "but I don't know why he quit us,"

"I know why," Dr. Tinterow said.

"Would you tell me?" I asked.

"It was the case you did for me at St. Joseph Hospital."

"I remember that well. The surgeon got lost, and I thought he was going to get in my airway in the neck." I had said nothing at the time, but Dr. Tinterow knew all about it.

"That surgeon knew that you knew he got lost," Tinterow explained, "and he said he would not use you again. I was not sorry to lose that surgeon."

A doctor friend named Bob Wilson told me that in the town of Osborne, Kansas—an area where his wife had lived—a doctor was looking for another doctor to practice. Zilpha and I had an apartment with belongings and two old cars, and we set out for Osborne. It was certainly lucky that I was well educated in medicine, because I sure was stupid about almost everything else.

I started practice with the other doctor on a more or less paid proposition. The doctor told me he was a surgeon—he wanted to be called a surgeon and an OB doctor. In reality, he was just a general practice doctor.

Our relationship did not last very long—less than a year. During the time I worked with him, I gave anesthetics for surgery, but his procedures were not acceptable to me. He did supra-cervical hysterectomies, and he took three hours to do them. I helped with some surgeries, and I gave the anesthetic for others. He went away on a vacation, and when he came back, he told me to leave.

There was a basic problem between us. It was that welfare did not pay for prescribed drugs. The older doctors dispensed their drugs from the office. If we prescribed, we had to pay the drugstore for the drugs out of the office call charge. This was easily handled. Just charge enough calls until it paid for the drugs. I guess it depends on how you look at it, but I looked at it as not ethical, and I said so. I said it had to stop, but it was because of this (and other things) that I was asked to leave, and I was not sorry.

I had become great friends with Earl Wooley, a banker. When I told him what had happened and said I was moving on, he said I could have any building on Main Street for an office if I wanted to stay. I found a building that I thought would be fine. It was next door to Raney Drugstore and was owned by the store. The owners wanted eleven thousand dollars for it. At one time it had been a grocery store and had a large area—eighty by twenty-five feet without partitions—and an eleven-foot ceiling. There was a second floor with a staircase in front, but the top floor was in shambles.

I grew up learning how to use my hands, so I decided to get the building and convert it into a doctor's office. I did a lot of the carpentry work myself, after hours. I had a fairly busy hospital practice, and I gave anesthetics. Very quickly, I put up the division between the front waiting room and the business office and one examining room. I built the partitions on the floor. I made them 1½ inches short. I then put them in place and set them on two-by-four blocks to put them up to the ceiling.

The building had a Celotex ceiling with lighting fixtures in place. It was three o'clock in the morning when a friend and I put the division up and nailed it in place.

The ceiling was not uniform, and the floor was not level. We shimmed everything in place. One of my friends looked at my work and said the studs were not plumb. "Nothing is," I told him, "but I'm going to cover it with sheetrock, so it doesn't matter." I practiced there fifteen years, and it did not matter. I used only single studs on the doorways. This was not correct, but it did fine. They were interior doors.

My practice grew slowly. I hired three people: a registered nurse, a receptionist, and a person to do tests. I had four major examining rooms and an office. In addition, I had a reception room, a business office, and a cleanup room with a sterilizer and sink. Then I eventually had an X-ray, lab, and treatment room.

Early in my practice, Earl Wooley told me to advertise for help, rather than seeking people to work. I have always used that procedure and also have had many apply when I needed help. The idea of advertising for jobs has worked out perfectly my entire career.

I have given a lot of thought to my relationship with doctors. Overall, I would classify my success with other doctors as very poor. I am certainly not proud of this, and I've given much thought to ways I could have done things better. At the time, however, I did my best. I certainly realized what was happening and that I wanted it to be better, but in spite of myself, I could not do any better.

In my relationship with my employees, I had great success. Over the entire forty years of my practice, I got along splendidly with my employees.

If they had a problem with me, they never said anything about it. I can only remember one confrontation with an employee. When my people were hired, I explained that their job was to do whatever I needed. One day, I asked an employee, my laboratory technician, to go to the storage area above the office and get a file.

"I wasn't hired for that job," she replied.

"You were hired to do anything I need," I reminded her, "but what's the problem?"

"It's dirty upstairs," she said.

I had not thought about that. She wore white clothes, and I certainly did not want her to get her clothes dirty. "I'm sorry," I said. "You are perfectly correct. I will go there after hours."

My relationship with the hospital was quite stormy. They seemed not to provide qualified people and seemed not to care. They were mostly interested in the bottom line of money.

I did not like useless tasks. One such task was called "utilization review."

In it, I was to review the reason for keeping the patient in the hospital.

The first question was, "Is the reason for continued stay justifiable?" Well, no one ever gave good reasons, and I got tired of it and stopped doing it.

The acting administrator and a nurse, came to me and asked why I was not utilizing charts. I said it did no good.

She demanded that I comply, and after a long argument, I relented.

The reason for continued admission on the first chart I received was that the bowels had not moved yet. That is neither a diagnosis nor a reason. I rejected it. The next thing I knew, the admistrator came and asked why I had rejected it.

"It's not a good reason for continued admission," I said.

"Did you read the chart?" she asked.

"No, I was to be given a reason, and that was not satisfactory."

"Read the chart," she instructed me.

"Let's both go and read the chart," I suggested.

The chart showed nothing unusual ,and had very little on it. I then handed it to the administrator to read, saying, "Give me the form." I wrote "accepted" across the form, handed it to her, and said, "Never bother me again."

These types of conditions made me decide to make things as good as possible. My main concern was the care of my patients, both in the office and the hospital. Instead of pointing out what was bad, I decided to help make things better. It started with my office practice in that converted grocery store building; over fifteen years, that bare start became a prosperous operation.

I had a wonderful relationship with Earl Wooley, but the actual president of the bank was Earl's father-in-law, Charley Glen. I was drinking coffee with some friends one day, when they began telling me things that one only would know from my financial statement that I had given the bank. I went to Earl and asked him what was going on.

"Charley took your statement to Mr. Garrison at the other bank," Earl explained. "Garrison is the president of the hospital board, and they discussed your statement and the other doctor's at the board meeting."

"That's easy to cure," I said. "I'll change banks and use Luray's Bank."

"Don't do that," Earl said. "It would hurt the bank."

"That is not important," I told him. "I don't have a lot of money."

"The cash flow is the important thing," he remarked, "and you are in the top ten in the town."

Later, when I moved, someone tried to harm me, and it was put out that I did not get along with the bank. It also was put out I did not get along with my church.

When we moved to Osborne, we attended an old clapboard Free Methodist church. It had a resident female pastor. My wife played the piano, and I led the singing. We were very active, and I supported it financially. The conference gave us a pastor, and the former pastor was left to run her two-building rest home. It was not long before we built a new church. The treasurer told me they could not have done it without me.

Someone also said I did not get along with the town in spite of the fact that I set up an industry, making a part for the company my father worked for. After this happened, it spurred another industry to start, and it still is in business today.

I made a good many friends and was part of a regular group who drank coffee together, including Earl Wooley, Marvin Leadabrand, and one or two others who were not regulars. The object of the group was to give each other a hard time. It was more or less an insult club. The more this was pushed, the harder we pealed out with laughter. Marvin was one of the best. He would laugh until his face was red. One time the Duckwall manager sat down and joined our group. I could see he was not taking our remarks well, so I told him we were kidding each other, and if it bothered him, he should sit at another table.

A young lawyer was a part-time member of the group. I was taking flying lessons, and it took me a long time before I could fly solo. He gave me the business about that. It was in good fun, and I took it with fun.

He had an airplane and had an accident. He landed short of the airport and hit the paved road outside the airport. He bounced, hit the fence surrounding the airport, and put a hole in the bottom of the plane. He bounced and then landed on the runway.

In one of our sessions, he was talking about the length of the runway and other particulars about the airport. He told me things I did not know, so I thanked him for his information, and then said, "I have a question—I really need to know this for my safety. Which runway has a post in the middle of it?" He did not appreciate my question as I had appreciated his information.

I attended regularly the circuit course given by the medical school. I was well into practice when Dr. Bolinger from the medical school came and gave a lecture that included a discussion of Kallman's syndrome. I had never known the name of the condition that I had, and I did not know about gonadatropin releasing hormone. After the lecture I went to him and asked if he remembered me from the endocrine clinics. He said he did, and I asked him what he thought if I told him I had absolutely no sense of smell. He said he thought I had Kallman's syndrome. I told him I wanted to prove it. I told him I did not have the tests available to me, but he did. I told him I would like to send blood after stopping my therapy.

He said he would like that. I did and the results were FSH 0 LH 0 and testosterone 0.

This made the diagnosis and I learned the name of what was wrong with me.

It was not long until I was put to the test. During my first year, a man called to say he thought his wife had shot herself. His wife had a spinal problem and was in a wheelchair. I took my nurse and all my anesthesia equipment in black bags and drove to the house.

I found the man's wife sitting up in the wheelchair with her head bent back; she was just grunting. She was cyanotic and had a bullet wound in her left chest. I was not used to this kind of situation, and I admit I was shaking. I intubated her, put her on a breathing bag and started breathing for her. I told my nurse, "Get an ampoule of epinephrine and give it to her in the arm. Then call the hospital to alert the other doctor and have them get the largest catheter they can find." I knew we did not have a chest tube. She lost an estimated five units of blood on the way to the hospital.

When we got there, the other doctor could see only what he thought was a sucking chest wound. He wanted to do what he was taught to do in such a case.

"I have positive pressure on the lungs," I told him. "I need a chest tube in the lower chest so that I can blow out the accumulated blood." He did this, and after blood was given, the patient began to flutter her eyelids and wake up. When I saw this, I bent over and said in a loud voice, "Did you do this?" She nodded her head.

I had no experience with bullet wounds, much less chest wounds, so I didn't know what to do. I decided to transfer her to Concordia, Kansas, where there was a chest surgeon. We called an air ambulance from Russell, Kansas. I left the endotracheal tube in place and put a large asepto syringe on the chest tube. During the trip, the bleeding drained into the asepto syringe. I forgot to get something to empty the syringe into, so I used air sickness bags. The pilot saw this and told me that blood is hard to get cleaned off an airplane. By the time we got to Concordia, the bleeding was very slow. The chest surgeon told me that if a major vessel is not severed, bleeding tends to stop when the lung is inflated. That was the first life I saved in my practice, with many more to follow. The patient is still alive after these many years

That trip in the air ambulance was my first airplane ride. During the trip to the hospital, I was busy taking care of the patient, but on the way back, I was able to enjoy the ride. What I noticed as I looked out was that most was that the horizon could tilt, but it seemed that I was straight up and down. That really bothered me. My only relief was to shut my eyes when the plane made a turn. At this point, it was not if I would learn to fly but when.

I was called late one evening to see the local Methodist pastor. When I got there, I noticed there were many bloody footprints leading to the bathroom. The preacher had a GI bleed and blood was everywhere. I got him to the hospital. We had a "walking blood bank," which meant we had the names and blood types of the people who were willing to give blood. I called the basketball game and asked for Earl Wooley. I told him we needed blood and gave him a list of people to find and send to the hospital. I had complete cooperation. In a very short time, we had six units of blood. I knew that one particular person who gave blood would be faint after the blood was drawn, so I put his feet up, gave him orange juice, and told him to just lay there, because I did not have time to worry about him. The next day the radiologist from Concordia and I did an upper GI series. The patient was lying on the table in the dark as we did our procedure.

Later, I heard him describe what had transpired. He said that it was dark and he heard a click-clack, click-clack. Then there was a light, and two doctors said, "Beautiful." The rest of the story was that both the other doctor and I wanted it to be a gastric ulcer. The click-clack noise was the registration of the film cassette. When the picture was taken, the fluoroscope screen lit up, and we could see the gastric ulcer in full relief.

We both were very pleased that an ulcer was the problem. I treated the patient vigorously for the ulcer, and he had no further problems.

My great friend Marvin Leadabrand, one of my coffee-drinking buddies, also had an ulcer. One evening, his wife called me and said he'd gotten out of a hot bath and fainted. I went to see him, and I thought he had a bleed, probably from an ulcer. He stabilized, so I followed him to see if he had a black stool. The next day, I told him, "My advice is that you get one bleed for free, but I'm starting intensive ulcer management." I used to tease him that I could follow him anywhere by his trail of DiaGel wrappers. "If you have a significant bleed again," I advised him, "you should have surgery." He did have another bleed, but when I wanted to schedule surgery, he refused. At that time, we did not have the drugs for controlling bleeding ulcers that we have now I told him that a second bleed was dangerous; any more might take his life. He paid no attention.

Some years later, he called me from Buffalo, Wyoming. He was on vacation and had a massive bleed. It took many units of blood to stabilize him. He said he was ready to come home and asked if would I fly up there and get him. I called the flight instructor in Russell, who had a Cherokee 6; we'd used it for the patient who had shot herself. Because he was teaching me to fly, he let me fly part of the way to Buffalo. I picked up Marvin, got him home, and scheduled surgery. Dr. Collier cut out the majority of his stomach.

Later, after I moved to St. John, Marvin called me and said he was sick. "If I come the hundred miles, will you see me?" he asked. When he came into the office, I could tell he was really sick, so I put him in the hospital. That evening, I looked at the lab work. He had an elevated calcium and an elevated serum protein. His differential blood count was not bad but troubling. The next morning, I did a bone marrow biopsy. I did a gram stain on it and directly looked at the slide. It was obvious that he had multiple myeloma. I made the diagnosis in less than twenty-four hours, but I waited for the pathologist to look at the slides.

I told Marvin, "I can't treat you, but I'll refer you to an internist in Beloit. It's my impression that treatment does not affect the outcome, but it does affect the quality of life and symptoms." Marvin survived for many years after that.

A patient's mother once stopped me on the street to say that her fourteen-year-old son was sick. "Would you see him?" she asked. It was not regular office hours, but I took him into a treatment room and examined him. He had a high fever. I noticed flame-shaped hemorrhages in the anatomical snuff box. I asked the mother how he got them. She said football. I then examined the abdomen, and those marks were on his abdomen. I then looked at the sclera, and there they were. He did not have a stiff neck, but I was alarmed. I got on the phone to Dr. Dowell

Weber in Salina, an expert on meningitis. He had been my teacher in med school. I told him about the patient and said, "I want to load him with penicillin and send him down to Salina."

"Don't use the antibiotic," Dr. Weber responded, "and don't let him go home. Tell him to come directly to Salina."

That evening, I called to check on the patient and spoke with Dr. Weber's partner. He said that a spinal tap had been done, and the fluid was clear. I thought, I guess he does not have meningitis, and Dowell told me the spun-down sample had white cells with gram negative diplococci in them.

This made the diagnosis. I said, "It is early. Please cure him." The response was that the last two they had with meningitis both died. My patient did not die; he is still alive.

I never liked to go to the scene of an accident. Quite often, the ambulance beat me to the scene and was gone before I got there, and then there was no doctor at the hospital when they arrived. In spite of my feelings, however, I would have had a public relations problem if I did not go. I was called to an accident in the rain. I recognized the patient, who had a lot of bleeding from her head. I spoke her name, and she answered me. I took a sponge out of my bag and wiped off her head. She had brain hanging out of the right front of her head. There was not an available ambulance, so we took her to the hospital in the back of a station wagon.

At the hospital, I did an assessment of the wound. I could put my finger behind her right eyeball, and a large piece of the skull on the right frontal region was missing. The dura also had a missing and shredded section. We cleaned her up and took her into surgery. I gave an anesthetic, and the other doctors started the repair. They certainly were not neurosurgeons—one of them used an ordinary suction and ended up sucking brain into it. I had to tell him to stop. Normally, suction on the brain is done through felt-like patches. they used the fascia on the side of he face to repair the dura, and they closed the muscles of the face over thewound, leaving her with a large soft area on her head. she survived, andI sent her to Wichita after she healed for plastic surgery repair. the bone below the eye was smashed, and the cheekbone was smashed. This made the eye drop down. People can adapt to variation in the position of the eyes from side to side but not up and down. In spite of all the work done by plastic surgery, the last time I saw her, she still had double vision. She said that she had to figure out which curb to use to step down.

This was one of many accident victims that I dealt with. A propane truck hit a car full of girls going to school. On impact, the gear shift lever was shoved into the chest of the girl in the front passenger seat. Paramedics had to saw it off at the scene, and she arrived at the hospital with a short piece of shaft sticking out of her chest. When it was forced into her chest, it went through the diaphragm, tore the spleen apart, and shredded the left kidney. The lever then shed the knob when it hit the vertebra and bent and a nib was sticking out the back. She had massive bleeding and was in deep shock. I had a lot of experience with shock but not that extreme. I tried to stabilize her, and we called Dr. Collier for the surgery—if she did not die before he got there. I could not get her blood pressure to register at first, but after a lot of fluid and blood replacement, her blood pressure was 70/40 by the time Dr. Collier got there. "I thought she wouldn't make it," he said.

"I thought she would," I responded. "You should have seen her when I started." We took her to surgery, where I gave the anesthetic. The surgeon entered the chest and opened the diaphragm. He then entered the abdomen and removed what was left of the spleen and kidney and controlled all the bleeding. The wound was repaired, and the girl survived the surgery—the end result was, she survived.

In another car accident, one of my patients was severely torn up. She was one of four, but I took her into surgery and left the others for the ER. I counted twenty-seven fractures. She had a fractured femur, which I stabilized in the surgery. I put a pin through the distal head of the femur and put her in traction. We had only one traction splint, so I asked the hospital workman to make me a plywood ramp to support the femur for the traction in the hospital bed. I left the splint for the other doctors to use on other injuries from the accident. My patient also had a fractured jaw, right through the center of the lower jaw in the front. I could see both ends of the bone, and some of her teeth were broken out. She was unconscious and remained so for five days. After she woke up, I called the local dentist, and we wired her teeth together. He pulled a broken front tooth to aid in breathing. When the teeth are together there is not much room for breathing. She eventually stabilized, and I then got Dr. Yost from Nebraska to come and put an intramedullary pin into the femur to stabilize it. At that time, I asked him to evaluate the pelvic fracture.

He advised, "Tell her that if she has a baby, she should not have a vaginal delivery." I did so, and the end result was that she got better and left the hospital. I did not see her for a long time, but much later, she came into the office with a very young baby. I was curious to know how her delivery had been handled. She said, "I told the doctor what you said after my accident, but he said he doubted your advice. Then he took an X-ray, and when he saw it, he said 'C-section.'"

Over time, I set up an office laboratory. I decided to do cultures. I made up plates and did cultures for beta hemolytic strep. I did a lot of these but did not find much strep that I could worry about. Then one day, I had five in a row from third-grade kids. One of my former office nurses had become the school nurse, so I got some kits from the state, and she helped me send in cultures from the entire class. It had a very high percentage of strep. Dr. Charbaneau was the public health officer, so we contacted him and suggested we culture the whole school. This was done, and a large percentage was positive. I recommended penicillin treatment.

After this was done, I recultured my patients to see who might still be positive. I got a 15 percent recurrence. The doctors at Smith Center found out what we did, and one of them called me. He said, "Treating carriers is not recommended."

"I know that," I responded, "but school was about out, and if I cut a swath through the carrier base, the fact school was dismissed would take care of the carriers of strep."

"I didn't think of that," he admitted. "That was a good idea."

I then got a call from the state, asking if I was the one responsible for sending in seven hundred tests. When I said I was, the person calling said, "Do not do that again!"

"I won't," I assured him. I wanted to make it a study, but I was not the public health officer, and I did not want to muddy the water between us.

The country had a program to stamp out polio. On one day, all across the country, doctors gave Sabin vaccine on sugar cubes. I called the March of Dimes women in Osborne and asked what they were going about the stamp out polio crusade. They said the medical society rejected the plan to do anything. "I will help," I said. "If you work things out and get the vaccine, I will back you, medically." These women were the prominent women in the town. Everything went fine, and we made plans. Suddenly, the leader of the March of Dimes called me to say there was a problem.

The medical society had heard what we were doing and were scheduling a clinic one week before the one we planned. I said, "That's simple. Why don't you call Dr. Henshal and ask him if we can help? Say that we have a lot of people who can help."

"You would do that?" she asked.

I said, "The only thing we want is to stamp out polio. Who cares who gets the credit?" I took a bunch of vaccine to Downs and Natoma.

I did get to write some papers regarding medicine and publish them in the state journal. I saw a patient in my office for a routine physical. I notice he had only one testicle, and I asked him how that had happened.

He said he had a seminoma, and it had been removed. I then saw his breasts also had been removed. He told me they were enlarged and were removed because the size had bothered him.

I walked down the hall and told my nurse I thought he was doomed.

"I think he has a germinal cell carcinoma that's producing agents to enlarge his breasts," I said. "I think the cancer was not completely removed."

However, if I told him that, I knew it would really shake him up. Without further evidence, I decided to say nothing but watch what happened. Eight years later, he came in because he thought he might have appendicitis. I examined him, and his pain was retroperitoneal. I told him I wanted to do a test. I sent in a quantitative Friedman; it was very high. This test is a measure of the hormones that caused the breast enlargement. I sent my patient to the med school at Kansas University. They found a mass by the patient's kidney.

KU sent him home after radiation treatments. Some time later, he had a seizure and fell out of bed. I did an X-ray and found masses in the chest. I called KU for a recommendation. The doctor with whom I spoke said there was nothing more to do. I asked, "Do you know about the use of Furacin for these tumors?"

"It's experimental," he said, "but you can try. You would have to be in a protocol."

I wrote the company and found out my patient qualified. I started the medicine. It did not work. Although there was some improvement, he died.

I wrote it up for the journal, and the publisher said that he would print it. After some time, when I didn't see my work in the journal, I called to ask why it was not printed. He said my style was "wrong." I said, "You have my permission to change it." The journal then printed it, but I could see no changes. Since the test that was high is sometimes used as an indicator of pregnancy, I like to say I am one of the few who diagnosed pregnancy in a male.

The hospital at Osborne had twenty beds. I worked hard to set up something like an ICU. It was not actually an ICU, but we called it "special care." It was a room much like the nursery, with a window visible from the main nursing station. When I performed my first successful CPR, I wrote about my setup and success in an article, and it was published in the state journal.

I had an OB practice in my office, and I delivered my share of babies.

It was my procedure to set the demand anesthetic machine to 50 percent nitrous oxide, and let the mother breathe as much as she wanted. I was the only doctor who did this procedure. It caused the mother to have analgesia and confusion. I was especially sensitive to those in the medical profession, such as nurses, and I took care to deliver without pain. One of the really nice nurses was under the other doctor's care but delivered when he was gone, so it was left to me. I delivered her, and she was very grateful.

She said she had not chosen me as her doctor because I shouted at my patients in delivery. What she did not know was that I shouted because I needed the patient's help, and the nitrous made it difficult for her to hear me. She thought I hadn't shouted at her, but she was wrong. I had shouted loudly at her, because she used a lot of the gas.

Another very nice nurse was delivering with the other doctor, and she was making a lot of noise. I did not like it, so I went into the operating room, took the big anesthetic machine, and started giving her gas. I just gave her enough to confuse her but not enough to affect the delivery of the child. The baby delivered, but she was confused from my anesthetics and kept yelling, "Who does it look like?" I could not resist; I said, "The baby looks like me." Later, when she went back to work, she stopped me at the nursing station and said, "I told my husband, Paul, what you said, and he said he would love the baby anyway!"

A young mother who went to my church asked me to handle her pregnancy. It was baby number five. Baby number four had been spontaneously delivered while she was sitting in a wheelchair in the hall of the hospital. Now, she was eight months' pregnant and feeling twinges.

She was concerned because of the previous birth. I examined her at the hospital. She appeared to have a transverse lie, and it alarmed me. I felt she was in danger, but at only eight months, I did not want to do anything, as her situation could well change. I thought I might take her to Smith Center to see if they could do anything that I could not do. I went to get my station wagon that had a gurney in it. When I returned, I detected she was in labor—I had worked so closely with my OB patients in school that I could tell by just looking—and she said she also thought she was in labor. I then did a sterile pelvic to see the condition of the cervix, and I had an arm in the vagina. She was in labor and had a shoulder presentation, which is an impossible delivery. She was a member of my church so we prayed together.

I called out the surgical team and scheduled an emergency C-section.

I prepared a table where I could handle the resuscitation of the baby after delivery. I helped up until the time the baby was delivered, and then I took her to the table. She was not breathing or gasping, but she had a heart rate of 140. I did not have a tube small enough, so I cut the tip off the red rubber catheter and threaded it into the baby's trachea. I used my mouth and gave respiration. It lasted for fifteen minutes. Those at the operating table kept asking if the baby had taken a breath, and I'd say, "Good heart rate but no breathing." Suddenly, the baby started gasping and then breathing. That was over fifty years ago, and a couple of years ago, I visited Osborne and got a big hug from the lady who had been that baby.

Later, when I was in Fritch, I was just entering the hospital when a nurse grabbed me and said she had a patient in the delivery room with no doctor; she was complete and needed me. I was not her physician and I was not on call, but I responded to the call of need. I scrubbed and draped and did the startup things, and then I put my hand in and examined the vagina. I shook hands with the baby. This was another shoulder presentation. This was the second time this had happened to me. The difference was, there were many doctors and surgeons available. I yelled for help, and soon an OB doctor, stuck his head in and asked what I had. I told him an impossible vaginal delivery, and he said, "Wait a minute." Well, I stuck my hand up high and took the pressure off the delivery until he could come and take her to surgery. I never saw the woman again. I have always wondered what the nurse thought she felt, saying the patient was completely dilated. Maybe she did not know what a hand and arm felt like.

I originally did not have an X-ray machine. One day, a seven-year-old boy came in with a midarm fracture. It was obvious. I sent him over to the hospital for an X-ray and asked to be called when the X-ray was ready. I then forgot about it. I was closing for the day when I suddenly remembered.

I raced to the hospital, and there he was, out in the waiting room. The X-ray had not been taken. I was very unhappy. The administrator said, "We set the priorities and will decide when an X-ray is taken."

"That is unacceptable," I said, "and if your priorities do not change, I will get a machine."

Tahe administrator told me, "You cannot get one."

I said, "Watch me!" I called Johnny Heller the GE salesman and asked him about it.

Johnny said, "There's one in Hoisington that's just right for you. I'll bring the important parts, and you can go get the rest."

It worked out just fine, and Johnny helped me set it up. He said I needed a 10 KVA transformer on the pole, dedicated just to me to supply the X-ray machine. When I went to the hospital, I looked up on the pole and saw a 25, which seemed to me to be too small. When my transformer was put in, I mentioned it to the men who installed it. The next time I looked, it said 35. I told the men that I must have been mistaken. They said I was correct, but they looked and changed it, and when they did, the leads came out in their hands meaning the transformer was damaged.

We had been having trouble at the hospital, but after that, the X-ray performed perfectly.

From that point on, I had an X-ray machine, and I took many X-rays over the years. I taught my lab worker to take the pictures, and she eventually became better at it than I was. I had to read a lot in order to be able to understand exactly how it worked and exactly how to use the machine. When I left Osborne, I took the X-ray tube away so no one could try to use it and hurt themselves.

I left Osborne for St. John, and I sold my building to Hays Mental Health. They had a very good business in Osborne and eventually built their own building.

The fifteen years I practiced in Osborne were my most active years.

When I went to St. John, I no longer gave anesthesia, and I no longer did surgery. I assisted on some cases with surgeons from Great Bend, and I still delivered babies, although not too many. I had an office, owned by the hospital, across the street from the hospital. As in Osborne, I had a satellite office in a town fifteen miles away, Macksville.

St. John had a wonderful ambulance service with EMTs; Macksville wanted one. They asked for help from St. John, but it was denied.

Someone from Macksville asked me if I could help. "We're trying to get an instructor from the program," he said.

I said, "I know the one who runs the program at the medical school." I called him, and he gave me a list for the Macksville people to choose from.

Next the Macksville people asked me to handle the medical part of the instruction. They provided a book to use, and it took about six months of weekly instruction. I did my part, and a group of EMTs graduated from the program. After that, I was popular in Macksville, so I bought a satellite office across the street from the school. I really enjoyed the practice there.

It was away from the politics of the practice in St. John. I practiced in St. John from 1975 to 1983.

From there, I went to Fritch, Texas, after I got my licensure straightened out. The practice was a basic wind-down from what happened in Osborne and St. John, but it started a new phase, and that was the start of working as a doctor in emergency rooms for Southwest Medical Associates.

I still delivered babies and delivered quite a few at my Fritch location.

One new thing was that I started seeing cases of STDs. It got so prevalent that I had to go to my lab person and check the diagnosis. I finally concluded that since we were fifteen miles from Borger, we were getting patients who wanted to keep the problem quiet. The only problem was that none ever complained of having an STD; I had to figure it out.

I was going into the Borger hospital one day when a nurse came running out. She said, "A patient is delivering in an ambulance! Come quick!" By the time I reached the ambulance, the baby was well on the way. The patient kept repeating, over and over, "Oh, shit!" All I could say was, "Not now, lady. Not now." The baby came quickly, and everything was okay. A few years later, I saw that lady again. She approached me to ask if I remembered her. I didn't at first—but I did after she reminded me of what she'd said on delivery.

It was in Borger that I devised a system to stop walk-in deliveries, and it also stopped our needing to send the babies to specialists after delivery.

I practiced in Fritch from 1983 to 1986, when I went to Electra, because Panhandle Rural Health did not renew my contract. I was not sorry about that, and the Borger hospital closed for one year after I left—it would have been very bad for me if I had stayed.

It was in Borger that I started my adventures in emergency room work for Southwest Medical Associates. This was new to me. I was exposed to patients with injuries that sometimes were quite severe. One young Hispanic man caught his hand in the saws of a cotton gin. He came in screaming. I did everything to help his pain that I could, but nothing helped. We were going to send him to a center for hand surgery, but I needed to do something first. A nurse anesthetist at that hospital showed up just then. I had given the patient Demerol with no results. She said I should give more, but when I did, it made him wild, which I'd known would happen. She then wanted to give Versed. I didn't agree with that but knew it would not hurt. Nothing happened. She then decided to paralyze him with Anectine. The helicopter was on the way, and the paramedics knew how to manage this. I did not agree with her, but if I'd objected, I would have problems with the hospital, so I said okay. The problem was, the Versed would keep the patient asleep until it wore off. Then the patient would awake paralyzed, but no one would know it, but he would.

I had given Anectine one time with the patient awake, and it was not a good thing to do. I caused no harm, but it sure scared the patient.

On the other hand, a nurse's husband—a farmer—caught his right arm in the baler. The machine practically tore his arm off from his body.

I could put my gloved hand under the muscles of his chest, clear to his sternum. His reaction was that he wanted me to put a Band-Aid on it.

Electra was very stable, and the practice was not very busy. The hospital, on the other hand, was trying to get things going. The end came when I became sick in 1989 and was told I had multiple sclerosis. I moved to Lubbock in 1990 and became the medical director at Lubbock State School. The practice of medicine was entirely different. I did not deliver babies, and I did not have much acute care. I did a lot of administrative work, which was what I wanted, as I did not know what was going to happen to me. I still worked the emergency rooms in small towns on my time off.

In 1993, I moved to Morton, where the practice was quiet—no deliveries, no surgery, and mostly internal medicine. It was the first place I learned about the physician's assistant. All this time, since Fritch, I had been working, at times, in the ER for Southwest Medical Associates. My contact was Gwen, the wife of one of the owners.

In Morton, the practice was fairly quiet and at a slow pace. We had a typical small-town emergency room, for which I was on call half the time.

One of the problems with the small-town emergency room was that the lab was shut down at night, so if I needed tests or X-rays, it would take hours to get them. This was my problem when a prominent man turned up with his wife, complaining of flank pain. He was semishocky, and his pain was troubling. He did not have a Cullen's sign with flank staining.

My feeling was that the differential boiled down to a kidney stone or a dissecting aneurysm. I have seen a number of dissecting aneurysms, but I have never known one o mine to survive. I needed tests, but I did not have the time to waste. I discussed this with the patient's wife. If I called the emergency helicopter, and the patient had a kidney stone, I certainly would have egg on my face. I decided to go for broke, and I called Lubbock.

In my conversation, the doctor on the other end started asking what lab results I had, but then he very suddenly stopped and said, "I guess that doesn't make any difference. I have a flight in the air. It'll be at your hospital in ten minutes." True to his word, the helicopter arrived, and the transfer went smoothly. In the operating room at Lubbock, the doctors found a dissection aneurysm and repaired it. His wife still gives me credit for eight more years of a good marriage.

The practice in the emergency room was where I got my inspiration for medicine. I had the privilege of saving lives and repairing injuries. I had to understand lab work and X-rays. I enjoyed doing this, and Gwen enjoyed sending me out to do the work.

She sent me to work the ER. An eighteen-year-old came in after a fight; he'd been stabbed in the chest. It appeared he'd been stabbed directly into the heart. He was unconscious and breathing badly. I put in a nasal tracheal tube and started breathing for him. I then assessed the stab wound. I thought he was having a cardiac bleed into his pericardium.

I was just starting to put in a needle to drain the pericardium when a surgeon came in. He wanted to put a chest tube in place. I felt that the stab wound was in the midline and not in the pleura. I let him put the chest tube in, and then I made him aware that the EKG showed the heart rate to be 35. He decided to take the patient into surgery, where he died.

The stab wound was directly in the heart.

In Borger, I was working the ER when a woman came in with a gunshot in the back. I stabilized her and called for the surgeon. When he came, he wanted to take her up to surgery, and he asked if I could help. I considered that a compliment and agreed. We opened the abdomen; there was blood everywhere. It was coming from behind the aorta. Suddenly, she had cardiac arrest. The surgeon asked me to do CPR. I said, "It won't work on a bled-out patient."

"She's young," he insisted. "It will work."

I administered CPR, and it did work, but she died. Later, the pathologist showed me a section of the aorta. It had blown out the back side of the artery and could not have been repaired in time.

In 1997, I had my final fuss with doctors, hospital boards, and administrators, and I retired. I had learned a lot about myself. I learned to deal with fellow physicians, and I finished the course.

CHAPTER 5

ENIGMATIC RELATIONSHIPS WITH DOCTORS

My relationships with doctors in practice started with the doctor in Osborne, Kansas. The relationship started out very well, but it did not take very long before I realized his values were not my values. When I started in Osborne, there were seven physicians in practice there. In Downs, Kansas, five miles away, there were Dr. Hardig, a self-proclaimed surgeon, and Dr. Hodgson, a very elderly physician. In Osborne proper, there were two older physicians, Dr. Henschal and Dr. Miller. Dr. Henschal barely had a practice, and Dr. Miller was basically retired. Dr. Miller had severe diabetes and had trouble seeing because of the diabetes. There were two osteopathic physicians in Osborne—a young Gene Charbonneau and his father. The osteopaths practiced out of a large frame house and did not use the hospital in the beginning. So when I started, I was the eighth physician practicing in Osborne County (if you could call the practice of the older physicians a medical practice).

The physicians who used the hospital were Dr. Cornely, Dr. Hardig from Downs, and me. Over the years, Dr. Hardig, Dr. Hodson, Dr. Miller, Dr. Henschal, and the elder Charbonneau died. Several physicians came to Downs, Kansas, and replaced Dr. Hardig and Dr. Hodson.

I practiced in partnership with Dr. Cornely for less than a year. I left him, purchased a grocery store building, and converted it into an office.

Later on, I set up a satellite office in Luray, Kansas. My relationship with doctors, at times, was very stormy. There were times they wanted to get rid of me, and they attempted to do so. I sincerely tried to avoid a fight and, for the most part, was moderately successful.

The first major battle was over the ability to do hip pinning on elderly welfare patients. We had a real problem. I wanted to do pinning in Osborne.

I was attending a fracture clinic when I noticed a young surgeon named Bill Collier sitting several seats away from me. I pulled up my chair close to him and started talking. I said, "The doctors in McPherson are not treating you well."

"What do you mean?" he asked.

I told him, "They are taking all the good cases in surgery and letting you have the scraps."

Bill nodded his head. "Yes, that's true."

"Would you come down to Osborne and do hip pinning for me?" I asked. "A fractured hip is an easy diagnosis, and I will prove to you that I can be trusted. I won't get you into trouble."

"I'd like that," he said.

I had my work cut out for me. I had to set up the operating room in a manner that would allow us to use the X-ray machine for the pinning procedure. I constructed a tunnel for the X-ray film to fit under the patient, so we could take pictures at the time of surgery. I had considered becoming a missionary doctor. It was for this reason that I assisted in many hip pinnings on my internship, because I felt it might be of use on the mission field. This allowed me to set up the situation at the Osborne hospital.

Dr. Collier started coming out to the hospital to do hip surgery. It started a long relationship between us. He branched out to do many other surgeries for us over the fifteen years of my practice there. After I moved on St. John, Kansas, I contacted him again, and he told me he'd stopped going to Osborne.

One of the other doctors wanted to be called a surgeon, but he certainly was not a surgeon like the ones in Wichita. He asked me to give an anesthetic on a patient with a second-degree heart block. It was an operation for a common duct stone. We never saw the stone, and it never was removed.

I considered the operation risky, from an anesthetic viewpoint. I asked, "Don't you want a big surgical team to do the operation in a larger facility?" He appeared to know everything about the heart problem and said, "It won't be a problem."

I still was very worried, so I intubated without stopping the breathing and used ether, because cyclopropane has a bad effect on the heart and circulation. Ether, on the other hand, will stop breathing before it causes cardiovascular problems. Breathing is easy to manage if the patient is intubated.

We were well along in the operation when I saw that the patient's ears had become dusky. The surgery wound was open, so I asked the surgeon what the blood looked like in the surgical field. He said it was fine, but at that point, the heart stopped—and it almost seemed that my heart missed a few beats also. My hands were full. I stopped the anesthetic, blew out the bag, and put the patient on pure oxygen. Meanwhile, the surgeon opened the chest and started massaging the heart. It started up again, but the blood pressure was all over the place. I had never taken a blood pressure like that before, and I have not since.

"We need to close up and see if we can get him into recovery in one piece," I told the surgeon.

"I'm going finish the surgery," he said. That really scared me, but I just did my best. About five minutes later, the heart stopped again. This time, the surgeon decided to follow my suggestion, and the patient was taken back to his room. He died five days later. Therefore, this was not considered an anesthetic death, I was having a problem adjusting myself to the type of surgery other family practitioners did. I had a hard time understanding why a family doctor wanted to be called a surgeon. I was accused of advertising, only because my name had appeared in an article in the newspaper. In response, I ran for the office of county coroner. I had many pleasant experiences in that position, but a few cases were very unpleasant. I had worked in close connection with the KBI and someone must have been pleased, because I was appointed as district coroner. Two experiences bring back memories of humor and angst. First of all, humor: I learned of a fight at Smith Center.

I knew the coroner at that town had a drinking problem. I wanted to be sure that a postmortem would be done, so I called the coroner. From the way he responded, he appeared to be intoxicated. I asked him about the case and told him I wanted a postmortem. I suggested he get Dr. Shepard to do the procedure.

"Dr. Shepard has already done the post," he responded. Then he added, "Dr. Shepard sent the head in."

Sometime later, I helped Dr. Shepard in surgery. I said, "You must do an unusual post to send in the head of a human. And if so, where do you send a head of a human?" Of course the head was not sent in. It was just the confusion of the coroner in Smith Center.

I had an unpleasant experience as a coroner. It was my practice to drive past the hospital before going home and check the cars around the hospital for information. You had in indication from the cars present and their condition whether an emergency was happening. This particular time, a car was in the emergency room drive with all the doors open.

There were no doctors' cars in the doctors parking lot. I went to see if I could help and found a dead child, with a nurse trying to breathe for it with the mask on upside down. This particular child had been admitted with a diagnosis of child abuse some time before. It was for this reason I made it a coroner's case.

The particulars were that the child had taken a massive dose of aspirin early that morning. I was concerned because of the past history. I called the KBI, and they came out to investigate the case. They reported to me that they could not determine the truth of matter. They suggested that I tell the parents to take a lie detector test, and if they would not, an inquest would be held.

The parents did not want an inquest, so they went to Great Bend and took the test. They passed, and it was over—or at least I thought it was over. The doctor at Downs called me and was very angry—he called me every name he could think of. It seemed He thought I was interfering with his relation to his patient. I was not doing this I just was following the advice of the KBI.

I was very active both in the hospital and in the town. I was made president of the chamber of commerce. During that time, I was involved in procuring a dentist for Osborne. He became my good friend, and I gave many anesthetics for him for dental surgery. It was later that he came to my office, and I led him to have Christ in his life. He told me that he later went on an evangelistic tour for Nicky Cruise and told the story all over South America about my leading him to Christ. He told me that I had many grandchildren in Christ all over South America—that pleases me.

One might think I left Osborne because of doctor relationships. That was far from the case. I basically left Osborne because of mistreatment by the hospital.

A good example of some of the mistreatment was the time when the hospital administration asked the staff to rewrite staff rules and regulations.

I objected; I could see no reason to rewrite a bunch of rules that were not being followed anyway. There was no real desire to break the rules; it's just that they were not practical. In general, the doctors did the best they could, and the breaking of the rules did not cause a serious problem.

However, so much pressure was exerted that I finally agreed to write a set of rules that agreed with the practices that were being done. I spent a good deal of time doing just that. I gave my rules to a man, who was a representative of the group that ran the hospital.

We had a meeting to accept the new rules and regulations. You must understand that I had no ax to grind. I really didn't care if they accepted my rules or not. The meeting began, and my rules were considered. All of a sudden, the representative came in with another set of rules for us to consider.

I will never know why he did not give them to us in the first place. I'd spent a lot of time working on new rules for nothing. I reviewed the rules he brought. I then said there was something that had to be changed. He bristled, thinking I was going to criticize his rules, but I had found a place in the rules where our hospital was referred to as the Smith Center Hospital. Since the hospital was in Osborne, Kansas, it needed to be changed. All he'd done was take the Smith Center rules and apply them to the Osborne hospital. He was not smart enough to be reasonable about what should be done. I was tired of all the mistreatment and decided to move to the town of St. John.

The treatment I received from the hospital in St. John was fair and just. I have no complaint with their treatment of me. The frustration I had with the doctors in Osborne taught me a lesson, so I tried very hard not to have hostility breakout. For the most part, I did a fair job of this, and although the other doctor wasn't happy with me, we really didn't have any fights.

I was drinking coffee with the county attorney, and he asked me if I understood the Darling case. "I have no idea what you're talking about," I said.

He said, "If one doctor knows another doctor is practicing badly and does not inform the hospital, that doctor is liable. I urge you to inform the board of the irregular practices of the other doctor." I had no idea what to expect, but I did what he wanted.

Understand that there were a lot of issues that could have caused the county attorney to ask me to talk to the board. The other doctor ordered massive amounts of physical therapy at the hospital—so much so that we had a registered physical therapist working at the hospital. He ordered lots of it. He saw how much the hospital was making from this and decided to hire the therapist in his office. He did a lot of physical therapy in his office, charging Blue Cross and Blue Shield. Blue Cross and Blue Shield would not honor the charges when they came from his office. He had a very large fee to Blue Cross Blue Shield that needed to be paid. He hired the county attorney as a lawyer to get the money. He lost, and I was told he did not pay his lawyer. I do not know if this caused county attorney to tell me what he did.

I did tease my friend the county attorney about this seeming conflict of interests and in spite of it, I decided to inform the hospital board.

When I met with the hospital board, I told them, as best I could, what was good and proper medical judgment and that it was lacking at times in the other doctor's actions. I think if the board could have taken me out and lynched me, I would not be writing this account now. I got out of that meeting, bruised and bleeding and hurting, so to speak. I decided I'd done my job, and it was up to them. If anything happened, it would be their problem.

The end result was that the inevitable happened. After a long fuss, the other doctor left, and when he did, things were not happy. I had been offered a job in Texas, but the sins of the past caught up with me. Those in the past were determined to give me trouble, and it took me a while to get a Texas license. I cannot say that the problem I had was not my fault to some extent. I do not blame those in the past for the trouble they caused me in getting a Texas license. I do blame them for the unfair treatment they gave me and the fact they knew of the problems of the other doctors and did nothing about it. As for St. John, the hospital no longer exists, and the only close hospital is at Stafford, Kansas.

I left for Texas after clearing the problem with my license, and from that time on, I had no problem with other doctors. I hoped I had learned my lesson of how to get along, and it appeared I had. In Fritch, at the Borger hospital, we had disagreements at times but no fighting. In Elektra, there was no problem between the doctors. At Lubbock State School, the relationship between the doctors was wonderful.

I only worked at Morton for three years. The other medical doctor at Morton did not like me, but I think he was more unhappy with the hospital administrator than he was with me.

I had gone on a vacation, and when I came back, I was told the other doctor was leaving. This was just before I turned sixty-five, and I'd told the hospital board I would not promise that I would not retire at sixty-five, so they should consider that before giving me a contract. They gave me a contract anyway.

There was a hospital board meeting the day after I returned from vacation. I went early to attend the board meeting and saw the hospital administrator sitting there, waiting for the board meeting. She asked me what I intended.

I said, "I will let the board know that I won't retire and leave them without a doctor if the other doctor leaves."

"He's not going to leave," she responded—and he did not. "He was just trying to get me fired, and he did."

"I guess I don't need to stay."

"After he finishes with me," she said, "he will start with you. Don't you want to protect yourself?"

"I have nothing to protect," I told her. It all happened just as she had expected. I left and did not attend a board meeting.

In my free time, Southwest Medical Associates asked me to work emergency rooms. I had stopped doing this when I started working at Morton. After consideration, I thought it would be nice for me to keep my hand in the work, in case I needed it in the future. I went to the administrator and asked her if I could do that on my free time, if it was consistent with my contract. She said there was no problem, so I scheduled some work on my time off. the other doctor found out I was doing this, and all of a sudden, the administrator was in my office. She said, "I know what I told you, but I'm having a problem. The other doctor said he wants you to stop."

"That's simple," I said. "I don't have to do it, but I need to fulfill a couple of obligations before I quit." I would not leave Southwest holding the bag.

After this happened, I decided it was unfair. What I did on my own time was my business, not the business of the hospital and not the business of the other doctor. Because of this, when I wrote a letter to the board regarding my new contract, I asked for the stipulation that I could do this on my own time and explained why I considered it fair. They had no problem with granting my request. However, when the blowup occurred and the administrator was fired, there was a big hubbub over my using free time to cover emergency rooms. The hospital board president called me to say I no longer could cover the emergency room of other hospitals.

"I asked to have this privilege," I told him. "You do not tell me I can't.

You can ask me if I would consider stopping, but I see no reason for you to command me."

I was my desire to retire. The problem I had was that my contract required that I give notice for a certain time before I left. I wanted to stop and leave immediately. If I had stayed the time required, my life would have been made miserable. I took my contract to the local lawyer; he told me it was a bad contract. He said he didn't know if I would be penalized if I left immediately. Then he charged me $160.

I wrote a letter to the board, explaining that I wanted to leave and trying to persuade them that it was all right. I was successful, and I was free from all the fussing that was being done. I really had no part in the fuss, but a lot of people thought I did.

I retired to Morton and still live there. For some time after I stopped working at the hospital, I worked for Southwest Medical Associates, covering emergency rooms. The entire time I worked for Southwest Associates, I had no conflict with them. They treated me with respect, and I had a wonderful time. One time they called me and said they were in a bind; they needed someone to cover Beeville, Texas. They flew me down there and chauffeured me to Beeville. I covered the emergency room, and then they did the same thing and returned me home. I felt like I had been treated like royalty.

CHAPTER 6

THE FIGHT WITHIN

Very early in my life, I faced what I was really like. Comedian Red Skelton used to have a routine where he played the little kid. He would say, "If I do it, I will get a whipping." Then he would say, "I do it!" I recognized that in spite of my will power, I was unable to keep from getting in trouble, just like the little boy.

When I was a child, attending a Free Methodist camp meeting at Downers Grove near Chicago, a leader in a children's meeting described just that problem. I went to our cottage and asked my mother about it.

She went to the leader and told her that I was spiritually hungry and to give me a chance to solve my problem. She did, and I applied the process and solved my problem.

I still was just like everyone else. I was a liar and a thief, but I had the power now to change my ways and overcome my natural inclinations. It did not stop the conflict, but I now had the power in my life to keep from destroying my life.

The end result of this experience started me on a quest to understand myself. It was quite a quest, because I had problems that created problems.

I was born without a hypothalamic messenger, which made me very slow to grow and left me with little to no physical strength. I went to doctor after doctor for the first seventeen years of my life. The doctors noticed that I had an undescended testicle, and that was all they could see. Now, doctors know that APL injections will make it descend. I had series after series of weekly shots for seventeen years and exactly nothing happened.

Starting shots before I was six years old caused a lot of fear. In addition, the fact that I was small and very weak made me target for every bully in the school. I have been asked if that caused me to have a psychological problem. It would be very hard for me to know.

What I do know is that starting at age six, I had asthma, and it got worse and worse. I went to the allergy clinic at the medical school, but no treatment helped. In addition, I wet the bed until I was in my teens. I had no idea why, but it was because my urogenital system was immature, and my bladder was very small. However, I was totally humiliated over the problem, and it really had no solution.

In grade school, the physical abuse was not severe; the teasing was severe. However, I have never had a problem with teasing. I am very articulate and can hold my own with anyone who takes me on. In grade school, it did not escalate to physical violence. In grade school, I had my first exposure to science. I took it in with great pleasure. Any time I could go to lectures on science, I was completely at attention. I became enthralled by electronics, and I constructed crystal sets. Just before high school, I received a chemistry set and from that time on, I lived and breathed chemistry.

I attended Rosedale High School. The junior high was in the high school, so I started in the seventh grade. This started a system of students laying hands on me. The students stood around and started grabbing each other's crotches. That started a system of physical abuse.

When I complained to the principal, his response was that I asked for it. I complained to my mother, and she said that if I would bloody some noses, it would stop. I remember sitting down and really thinking about these solutions. I decided that both my mother and the principal knew nothing. I decided I could stop it. I was not strong enough to take them on, but I could stop it with a baseball bat and surprise. They certainly deserved to be totally disabled. However, I reasoned that in spite of the fact that my teachers would do nothing, if I had taken action, my teachers would then do a lot. Therefore, I concluded that I would just put up with the physical abuse.

When I was in the eighth grade, I talked to one of our neighbors, Lowel Strong. He was several grades ahead of me and fit his name. He agreed to persuade my bully friends to lay off, and it helped a lot.

With my physical problems and the physical abuse, my plate was full.

The only thing I had going for me was my intellectual abilities. I did well in school. I had a principle that I used: every course I took, I wanted to completely understand. I had no interest in just answering the questions on a test. I wanted to be able to understand how everything worked and how things were related to each other. At that time, I took an IQ test.

My result was 120. It was a written test. Later, I found out that my test actually was a verbal IQ of 140 and a performance IQ of 100. I started on my quest to understanding myself.

In 1948 I entered school at Central Academy in McPherson, Kansas. I took seven solids and combined two years into one to graduate from high school. The abuse only got worse. I had several tormentors on the top floor of the dorm. The dorm proctor solved it by putting me in a room in the basement. That humiliated me. However, it was one of the first times that I learned that a little humiliation does not really harm anyone. It did, however, push me on to better understand myself.

I had a wonderful teacher who taught me history and civics. Her name was Rose Anderson. I sat and talked with her a lot. She told me something that I had already decided and that was to just endure the physical abuse.

She said I had a fine mind and that those I would associate with in the future would not resort to physical violence. She was so right, but I will never understand why those in control ignored the problems I had up until I was seventeen.

I graduated from high school at Central when I was just seventeen years old. I was a Christian, and I had been given power to exercise the determination to do the right thing. It was not easy, but a long time ago, I determined to change my attitude. It was working.

When I went to church, the preacher talked about the problem of making the right decisions and how it was a battle to do the right thing. He had an answer for that battle. It was called the experience of sanctification.

He did have me pegged. I was his best customer. The only problem was that what he said did not work. I remember that many times in my teens, I told God I wanted the fight within stopped, but if I had to wage the fight, I would do so. When he was ready to give me relief, I certainly would be ready.

It was solved eventually, and it is part of my understanding of myself.

It started in the summer before I started college. I had decided that I would be a chemist and that I would get a PhD. However, that summer I listened to a missionary doctor talk in church. A still small voice inside of me asked, "If that doctor died, would you be willing to replace him?"

I struggled with an answer, but I agreed that I would. I had no idea what that meant.

My brother was two years ahead of me in school. He was on the road to become a doctor. I, however, was not convinced that I should go to med school. I asked my brother to work it out so I could take the premed courses and still have all the chemistry and math I needed to become a chemist. He did a wonderful job of setting up my courses. I still thought I would be a chemist—I had my plans worked out to the last detail.

I did not like history courses, where all I learned was data. I wanted science. I needed a BA, however, to take the courses necessary for premed and also to take heavy science and math. To fulfill requirements for my BA, I took basic psychology, then abnormal psychology, then personality, then somatopsychology, and finally adolescent psychology.

In taking those psychology courses, I furthered my quest of understanding myself. The abnormal psychology course was pure Freud. I found the structure of this was a good way of understanding the mechanism of the mind. It helped me a lot to understand the basics of id, ego, and superego. I now had a system to understand myself.

I had spent seventeen years of praying about my problems. My asthma was solved when I was fourteen. I still had the problem of size and strength and the fear I might wet the bed, although it was under some control. As I mentioned, God solved my problem when I was seventeen. I grew, and my urogenital system matured. Now the God that had remained silent for so long suddenly had something to say. I was told that I had to give up everything that I had planned and become a doctor. Up until that time, it was only maybe; now it was either/or—either I decided to put my plans in an ashcan, or I would have no more of the master of my life. It was a very hard decision, and it was not sudden. I took my time, but I finally decided to discard all my plans and ambitions. I told God I would not be a very good doctor. His answer was that it was not my business to make myself a good doctor; it was his. People have told me that I was not a good doctor. When that happens, I just look up and say, "I told you so," and we both laugh.

I only applied to one medical school. That was Kansas University. I decided if God wanted me as a doctor, he could do his part. The important issue was the problem of the fight within that a Christian has and if it would be possible to have it solved. Well, it did solve that problem. I found out that the quest after the good things in my life could cause a great deal of problems for me. After all the striving on my own terms was gone, I no longer had that fight within. Scripture talks about self-denial, and I found out what it meant.

A long time into my career, I was in the town of Fritch. Texas. We were going to a Baptist church. A Sunday school teacher made the remark that he had a black dog and a white dog inside of him, and sometimes the black dog won, and sometimes the white dog won. I wanted to tell him I knew what he was talking about, and it could be solved, but I knew he would not understand.

Some of my earlier life helped in medical school. I had conquered the fear of shots and in doing so, I no longer had a fear of medical procedures.

This helped in being able to understand how people felt about having things done to them.

In college and medical school, there was no physical abuse. In college there were a number of students just like me, and we sat around and picked each other's brains. There was little to no concern of who was smarter.

Medical school was just the same. By the time I was in medical school, I was married and had a partner in my life, and that made a great deal of difference. I had someone to understand and someone to understand me.

Internship was no different. We had jobs to do, and there was little friction. However, after I went to Wichita to practice and do anesthesia until my draft status was settled, I began to again see conflict. Most of the conflict that occurred between doctors had to do with ego and money.

However, I was basically a person of no importance, so I went without opposition. I still was on the quest to understand myself, and the lectures I attended on hypnosis helped me understand more.

Then my draft status was solved, and I moved to Osborne, Kansas. I shared a practice with another doctor. That did not last long. I can hardly criticize that doctor, because I know what I would be like without the grace of God in my life. I have nothing to brag about. However, there was a lot of conflict. That doctor did not practice good medicine. His favorite procedure was a supra-cervical hysterectomy. I practiced in Osborne for fifteen years. After I left, that doctor lost his license to practice.

On my quest to understand myself, I now had the problem of how to handle a difficult doctor who appeared to be an enemy. I am sure the hospital was aware of the irregularities in the doctor's practice. Yet they gave him partial treatment and allowed him to work it out, so that my call schedule doubled. His also doubled, but he never paid attention to it, so I just was left covering for him. The hospital took no steps to change this.

I learned that it was not only other doctors; I found that hospitals and hospital boards also are very difficult. They also have a problem of ego and money. That was the final straw that made me decide to move. In the weeks after I left, Main Street shut down for part of a day and the merchants marched on the commissioners over the hospital and its practices. For a time, that hospital administration was given the boot. All those fifteen years of stress produced a lot of prayer over the problems, and as before, I really got little response.

The problem came to a head when I was listening to preaching. The preacher was talking about a Free Methodist preacher who was starting work in the South. He preached on the street corners. People would throw eggs at him, and he would just wipe the eggs off and go on. Right then, a still small voice said that I was not very good at wiping eggs off my shirt, so to speak. I sat in the pew and cried and vowed to change and do better.

Then, all of a sudden, I was told that the problem with the other doctor was to be solved. My response was that he was not a problem right then.

Within a week, the other doctor was in a psychiatric ward in the hospital in a larger city. He spent several weeks there and was much better when he returned. Solving the problem with the other doctor did not solve my problem. The hospital administration cut corners to make money, and I was not their favorite—they made this quite plain. They hired lab techs who knew little and had no experience, even though they thought they knew everything.

An example: when I realized that the hemoglobin values were incorrect, I went to the lab and asked how they were doing the test. I looked things over and told the tech that she was using a curve made for a 5cc instrument and doing the test with a 6cc method. Therefore, the results were low and incorrect. If someone pointed out a mistake to me, I would appreciate it, but she got very angry. The hospital would not give me proper people to help in OB. When a doctor delivers a baby, he is sterile, so he needs someone to do errands while he is scrubbed up. It should be a nurse who has experience. Instead, I was given just an aide. One time I looked back, and the aide had her hand in the middle of my sterile table. I said, "Get your hand off my table." She was in the process of fainting and ended up falling to the floor. The next day I was called in and scolded because I'd made her cry.

The results of that experience were that individuals were pretty good but the organization of the administration of that hospital was something else. I learned not to blame everyone for the problems a few caused.

In spite of bad treatment, I did many things for the hospital that were milestones in treatment. I got Dr. Collier to do surgery. I set it up so we could do hip pinning in the hospital. I gave anesthesia, especially on difficult cases. I worked out a cross-match board, so we could give blood.

I collected money so we could keep the X-ray doctors coming. I set things up for special care so we could do CPR, and I had the first successful CPR at the hospital. Since we were a small hospital, I wrote an article on my setting up the special care, and it was published in the state medical journal. I found out why we were having trouble with the X-ray machine and got the city to change the transformer on the pole.

In addition, I did many good things for the town. I started an industry based on a part my father sent me. I helped get a dentist. I worked things out to help the polio clinic stamp out polio. I converted an empty former grocery store into my office, and I set up a satellite office twenty miles south in the town of Luray.

I left Osborne because the hospital was mistreating me, and I had to do more coverage of the emergency room than was my share.

I met Bob Pearcy, who was the administrator of the St. John, Kansas, hospital. He was a great person, and I moved to St. John. There was another doctor in St. John, and on the surface he appeared to be okay. I moved into an office owned by the hospital and set up an office that I ran independently.

My experience with the doctor in Osborne made me wary of another relationship with a doctor. I had reason to be wary. It was not long before I had the wrath of the other doctor demonstrated. I had a very ill patient and wanted the patient close to the nursing station. the other doctor moved the patient without my knowledge. I told him that worried me, and he blew up and really reacted with wrath.

My reaction was to avoid conflict. I basically had no conflict with the other doctor. but when the county attorney told me I had to tell the board of irregularities in his practice, I did so. All I received was verbal abuse. That led me to assume I did my part. It was four years after that when everything blew up, but it did not involve me.

A nurse went to Rodney Lyons, who was a lawyer, and asked, "If I followed an order that was incorrect, could I be held liable?" He told her that yes, she could be held liable. The next time the doctor gave such an order, she refused to follow it. All hell broke loose. The hospital administrator and the director of nurses supported the nurse. It ended up in the newspaper. What I had told the board at the request of the county attorney now was in full view. I was playing in the orchestra at the community college in Great Bend, and some of the players would say they saw my name in the newspaper in the discussion of the fight with the doctor. My response was that it only said I was a staff member.

The head of the hospital board came to my office, but I never have figured out why. He stated that just because I said the doctor's practices were irregular, that didn't mean they would believe me. He said that they were getting Dr. Britton from Wichita to review his charts. The pharmacist who also was concerned pulled a bunch of charts for him to review. I heard a recording the pharmacist made, where the doctor was screaming over the phone at him. Dr. Britton was a good friend of mine.

I had on file some papers he wrote, including a particularly interesting one on the so-called Jackson's membrane disease. I gave anesthesia for him in Wichita. He was a doctor with a law degree. I was told he gave a very negative report on the doctor.

The problem was finally on the way to resolution when there was a confrontation, and it ended withthe doctor physically assaulting the administrator. He grabbed the administrator by his shirt front and pushed him into a wall.

The administrator was playing favorites. He was trying to get a young osteopath from Stafford to use our hospital. My feelings were to go for it.

I did not care if he was given partial treatment. He came to me and said we should kick the doctor off the staff.

"Do you know how hard that would be?" I asked him. "There is such a thing as due process, and it is difficult. Do you know what happened?"

"Yes, I do," he said.

"Did you see it yourself?"

"No," he admitted.

As chief of staff, I then suggested, "We should get a written account from a witness, and if happened as we think it happened, we can suggest a psychiatric work-up. If there was an assault, I can think of no mental reason why a doctor should do such a thing."

We had a staff meeting and recommended this to the hospital board.

The board took hold of it and told the doctor they would pay for him to have a review at Menninger's Clinic. This scared the doctor, and he obtained an injunction and resigned and moved. That did not solve my problem, however, as he had a great following. He'd prescribed a drug called Serax for almost every patient. Serax is a metabolic breakdown product of Valium and has identical properties. Half the town took this drug. After the other doctor left, they came to me to get the drug. I would not give it to them. No one ever told the true story of what I did, but I created a simmering, growing anger, and nothing good was being said about me. I was very unhappy.

At this time, I put out feelers to move. The family practice residency at Waco, Texas, contacted me and offered to hire me as associate director. I never had a residency but had taken the test and was board certified. They appealed to my ego, making me think I was the best thing since sliced bread. I have no idea why they thought I was so good. They hired me, and I went to Waco. They had a month-long course set up at the college to educate medical teachers. I took the course. When the month was up, the medical license board had not given me a license yet, so I called them.

I had a license in Kansas, Nebraska, Colorado, and Oklahoma, but the license board said that I would not get the license. I was devastated. My belongings were in a van ready for my move. I called my wife and told her to hold everything. It was over, and I was back in Kansas with the worst depression I ever had. I had no idea what was going on. I called again, and they said they thought I was emotionally unstable. I found out later that the hospital administration at Osborne had complained about me. They sent letters that I had written to them, complaining about my treatment. My banker friend said that I should have my fingers broken so that I would not write letters. I am not sure I ever learned this lesson, and I do not know why I do this when it is not good for me.

I decided that if I was unstable, I should be the first to know. I set up a psychiatric evaluation at Hays Mental Health Clinic. I told Dr. Cody my problem, and he put me through the wringer. I enjoyed every minute of the evaluation. I learned a lot about myself—it was a red-letter day in my quest to understand myself. I took the Minnesota Multiphasic Personality Inventory. The results showed that I was in good mental health and that I was equipped to do anything I set my mind to do. One thing I learned was that I thought I had more virtue than was true. Another thing was that I did not like to break rules. I put that to a test and found out that it was true. I had the findings sent to Texas, and they gave me a license, but the job at the residency was no longer available.

Not long after that, the residency at Waco had a big problem, and most of the people were fired, so I probably was better off.

Now I had to move. My house had only a few items; all the rest was packed up. We had a very large auction to get rid of a lot of the stuff. I started looking for work in Texas. I still had the other licenses too. I met with the administrator of the hospital in Borger, Texas, and was referred to a government-backed practice in Fritch, Texas. It was administrated by a young man, and there was nurse also in an office in Amarillo. The practice at Fritch was run by family practice residents out of Amarillo. It was offered to me, and I decided to set up practice in Fritch—the part-time residents no longer practiced there. I had indications that this did not make the residents happy, but they wanted me to start a stable practice. I practiced there from 1983 to 1986. Shortly after I arrived, the young administrator moved on, and I was left with the nurse running the office in Amarillo.

This arrangement gradually changed over the years.

During the time that I practiced in Fritch, I had a wonderful friend named Dr. Croll. He was an internist, and I sent many patients to him. I told him, "Anyone can run all the tests to decide what is wrong, but since you are an expert specialist, you are allowed only three tests to decide the problem." He was a good friend.

One day he called me and said, "The hospital wants me to work for Southwest Medical Associates and man the emergency room. I don't want to take both days of the weekend. Would you take one?" I agreed to do this.

I took Saturday, and he did Sunday. It worked out well. Then he decided to move on. Southwest Medical Associates asked me if I would be the director of the emergency room. This required my keeping track of who worked there and working out any difficulties. It paid a hundred dollars a month, and I really did very little work. This started a long relationship with the company, and I worked for them off and on, in various small towns, for years in my spare time. In the time I worked for them, I had the privilege of saving a number of lives.

I worked Herford, Texas, quite a few times. On one occasion, a very young child was brought into the emergency room, as limp as a rag and cyanotic. I put in place an endotracheal tube and started breathing for him. I looked up and saw a young male nurse. I asked him if he could put in inter-osseous lines. He said he could, and he put one in each leg. We gave a bolus of fluid challenge, and the child improved. I called for another bolus and in response, the child tongued the tube out of the trachea. I sent the child to Amarillo. Later, I called the pediatrician to find out how he was doing and what had caused the problem. He was stabilized, but they were unable to tell me the problem. Later, I went back to Herford and saw the male nurse—I referred to him as "super nurse." He told me that the problem was caused by the mother giving the child an adult dose of NyQuil.

While in Fritch, I set up an OB practice designed to eliminate the walk-in cases at the Borger hospital. One day I was talking with a nurse in the hospital about this, and I said my idea was to notify indigent patients by a notice in the newspaper that we would start their OB care in my office. When they came in, I would work them up and send them to the hospital to get them qualified for Medicaid. Then, when they came due, I would deliver them. It worked out splendidly. For a year, we had no walk-in patients, and the nursing director was very proud of the work we did. However, it did have a snag. There is a condition in obstetrics called intrauterine growth retardation. In order to avoid this, we had to diagnose it, which required two ultrasound examinations. These were performed at the hospital and cost a lot of money. The hospital had purchased an ultrasound for The OB doctor. I asked him if I could get it done at a more reasonable price in order to save money for the office. I worked for Panhandle Rural Health, and they paid for the procedures done on the patients. Well, I did save a lot of money. When the OB doctor quoted me a price, my response was, "I send you a lot of patients. Can't you give me a better price?" That really helped me out, but in the long run, it was not help.

A patient got mixed up and went to the hospital to get the procedure.

The hospital found out I was doing the procedure with the OB doctor. They were very angry; they wanted the money. Nobody gave me any credit. It was no skin off my nose if the procedure cost a good deal for the company.

I was having trouble with Panhandle Rural Health. They kept me on tenterhooks, waiting to know if the practice was funded. In addition, my contract had run out, and they made no attempt to produce a new contract. When I asked for one, they said, "What do you want in the contract?"

"Offer me one," I told them, "and I'll decide whether to accept it."

I do not think that sat very well with the nurse who was running the program. The next thing I knew, my services were terminated.

I was not sorry, but I did not understand why this had happened. I put out my feelers for other positions. The state medical society president flew to Fritch and asked me to come to his town to see if I would consider moving there. An administrator from Elektra, Texas, drove to Fritch and offered me a job at Elektra. I decided to take the job at Elektra, and in 1986, I moved to Elektra, Texas, and practiced there until 1989.

I do not consider the time spent in Fritch as contentious or difficult.

I basically had no problems with any of the doctors; the only problem I had was over doing ultrasounds at the OB doctor's office. I had no idea why I had to move. However, one year after I left, the hospital shut down. Of course, I had no part in that happening, but had I stayed, it would have devastated my practice. I considered this a providential occurrence. All things considered, I got a better handle on understanding myself.

The practice in Elektra had two doctors at the time. The administrator was not happy with those two doctors and not long after I came, they moved on to practice in Wichita Falls. That left me alone in the town, but those two doctors still lived in Elektra. They pulled a lot of patients to their new practice. The hospital had a rather aggressive program of promotion. I was practicing in a clinic by myself, and the hospital decided to build a clinic on the hospital. The young man who had worked the emergency room decided to set up his practice in the clinic at the hospital.

I decided to buy a building and set up a private practice. This seemed to be working out, although the practice was rather slow.

One day I was sitting in a chair at home, and the room started spinning. It was obvious that I had nystagmus. I thought it was probably positional, so I got up to see if it would go away, and I fell flat on the floor. I waited a while to see if it would stop. It was making me sick to my stomach. My wife was not at home, so I crawled to the phone and called for an ambulance. I had nystagmus for three days. A neurologist in Wichita Falls diagnosed me as having multiple sclerosis. This ended my family practice for the most part.

I decided I needed a position I could work at as long as I could, even if I had a disability. I put my feelers out and found a job at Lubbock State School. I was hired as the medical director. It was quite an experience. I went from a practice, where I was seeing private patients, to the management of a four-doctor group, who took care of patients who had an IQ below 80.

I had a lot of fun taking care of them and managing the other physicians in the care of these patients. I worked at Lubbock State School from 1990 to 1993. I had a lot of sensory problems, but I had little to no motor symptoms. I decided that it was unlikely I had multiple sclerosis, and I could risk getting into private practice again.

The state settled a significant lawsuit, and it resulted in a cut in the amount of money set aside for the state school. I was highly paid in comparison to the other workers. I felt it was only a matter of time until they needed me to leave, so I looked for something else. I was told that a rather large pay was available at Morton, Texas. I called the administrator and said, "A doctor cannot make that much money in Morton."

She said, "I know that, but there are problems, and if you could come and take half of the emergency room, and you are competent, we will be ahead, even if you do not see a patient in the office." I never heard anything so reasonable, so I went to see her. I was very pleased with what she had to say and decided to move to Morton and start practice in 1993.

I retired at age sixty-five in 1997.

Morton had a physician who was younger than I, as well as a physician's assistant (PA). The PA was named Pat Roper, and he was a wonderful guy.

I really enjoyed working with him. On occasion, he did things incorrectly, and I would tell him how things worked. Some time later, he would tell me he looked it up. That really pleased me and made me feel he was quite competent. He said he wanted to work the emergency room, with me as backup.

I said, "I don't need you. I've worked the emergency room 50 percent of the time all of my life."

"I want to work the emergency room," he responded.

I said, "I can understand that. I will work out an arrangement. Every case you have under my supervision, you will call me and tell me what you have. If the problem needs me, I will be right there."

We had a wonderful time working together. I began to think that I wasn't so bad after all in my relationships with other medical personnel.

However, that was to change. Later, we got another PA. I told him about the arrangement I had with the PAs. He complained to the other physician about it, and suddenly, I had a situation that could end in with a fight on my hands. I had to decide what to do. I remembered the Scripture that said, some men trust in horses, some in chariots. It basically stated that a person, regardless of how he tried, could not protect himself completely, so I decided to let it slide and crossed another hurdle of understanding myself. However, they did not leave it with that. The other doctor would leave town and leave his patients to the PA, without telling me anything about the patients. This caused me great concern, but I knew in whom I had my trust.

After the other doctor left, leaving his patients to the PA without any information for me, the PA then left. Someone had to see the patients. I reviewed the charts but received no help, so I started to see the patients and do a thorough exam on each one. When I saw the first one, I started to examine the cranial nerves and found her to have a third nerve palsy.

This was the first time I was able to demonstrate this on a patient. I was alarmed, and I called a neurosurgeon in Lubbock. I sent her to Lubbock, and he immediately took her to surgery. She had an epidural brain abscess.

It was this case that made me decide that if it had been the only success I had, it would have been worth my entire career. It also was a culmination of understanding myself, and as Paul Harvey says, that is the rest of the story.

CHAPTER 7

A HOME AND A FAMILY

My father met my mother at a little Free Methodist church on Southwest Boulevard in Kansas City, Kansas. They got married and lived with his family in their home until he had enough money for he and my mother to be out on their own. German sons gave all the money they made to their mother until they were married. They then lived in the family home and saved their money until they could be out on their own. During the time my mother lived with her in-laws, she learned that Germans thought American wives were lazy, and she learned German very fast so she would know what they were saying about her. She was not happy, and after Dad and she went out on their own, she did not socialize with the German branch of the family.

It was custom that the German families ate together on Saturday night. They generally ate sauerkraut and frankfurters. My mother told my father he was American, so this did not occur with our family.

I had three siblings. My brother is three years older. I had a brother, four years younger, who died at eighteen months of age from post-vaccination encephalitis from a whooping cough shot. He died twenty-four hours after receiving it. I had a sister, eight years younger than I, who died at age forty. I sent her to a neurologist and told him she had MS. He said she did not. He was wrong, and she died of the disease. The only ones left now are my brother and me.

I married Zilpha Dickinson in August 1954. We moved to the trailer in a trailer park south of the medical center and set up housekeeping.

Zilpha was teaching second grade at Shawnee Grade School. She went to work in a carpool. We did not have a car, so I walked the three blocks up Rainbow Boulevard to the medical school. We slept on a fold-down couch that was very small. It didn't seem to bother us, and I enjoyed having someone to love.

At the writing of this book, we have been married fifty-eight wonderful years. We have never had that an argument or fight. If we had, it would have ended in my wife just crying. I never could stand to see her cry, and I never caused her to cry more than once or twice.

When I was in medical school, my wife taught school and earned money for us. I worked in the summers at Midwest Research Institute and helped with the income. We did not have any financial troubles, even though we did not have a lot of money. On finishing my internship, we sold the trailer and moved to Wichita, Kansas, where I had a practice and gave anesthesia. We lived in a small apartment, and it didn't bother us at all. We were deeply in love, and it would not have mattered what our accommodations were.

When my draft status was settled, we moved to Osborne, where I started my first practice of fifteen years. After I constructed an office in old grocery building, I used my wife for my office girl. I did not hire other workers. The school superintendent came and said he needed a teacher more than I needed a receptionist. So he stole her from my work. I then had to hire someone to replace her, and at that time, I hired a registered nurse also. My wife taught school for several years, until we found it possible to start adopting our family.

At family camp, we talked to a preacher who had used the Home of Redeeming Love in Oklahoma City to adopt a boy. We contacted this agency and through negotiation adopted our first child. We named him David. Four years later, we decided we wanted a girl. We called the home and asked them to try to find a girl. We decided to call her Mary. It took a while, and I used to call to find out the progress. My answer was, "We have plenty of Marions but no Mary." Finally, in January 1966, we got our little girl. Now our family was complete.

My relationship with my parents and my brother took a strange turn.

I told my mother that she could tell me when my brother, Irvin, and his wife visited, and we would come and all get together. I was told that Lois, Irvin's wife, told my mother that she did not want me there when they were there. My mother agreed with her, but I do not know why. I wrote Lois and apologized for offending her and told her I would do my best to make things right. She replied that she had Christian love for me, but I was obnoxious, rude, offensive, and overbearing. She did not want to be around me, and she did not want to expose her son to me. I really did not know her, so I have no idea why she took that attitude.

My brother got in with a bunch of know-it-all religious people when he was in college. He stopped going to the church we grew up in and had extended discussions with my father on the Bible. At one time, he stated he thought my folks were going to hell. He married a woman of like belief. He considered himself an expert on the Bible; I have a rambling commentary he wrote on the book of Matthew. This caused my father great concern. My father fasted for one week and said he had a vision. This appeared strange to me. He said he saw my brother in a casket. I did not understand what it meant, but now I think it was to tell my father that my brother was spiritually dead.

My views are different from most of my friends. I do not believe in a literal interpretation of the Bible. I think there are two things. One is what the Bible says, and I have no problem understanding that. The other is what it means, and I have a hard time with that. I must not be trustworthy, because I am informed on the meaning only on a need-to-know basis, so I cannot go on and on about Scripture after Scripture and explain them. My information on meaning does not impress any of my religious friends. My take on that is that it was not for them anyway; it was for my individual need.

Things seemed to go along fine, and my practice grew. I did not make people wait in my office because of my experiences with waiting in the doctor's office. For this reason, the entire town thought I had no patients.

They could see through the door in my waiting room, and it would be empty. The money from the practice, however, made home life extremely pleasant. I bought a house, I bought cars, and I built a satellite office in Luray, Kansas. I was living the good life.

I had a large practice. I incorporated and had a profit sharing pension fund.

Then I found out that Paul Yardy a Free Methodist missionary to India wanted to come to the U.S. to educate his children. A still small voice got my attention.

It told me that I should write him and offer to trade him my situation even up and agree to replace him. I should give him my office, my bank acount, my house, my car and trade him. I told God that I liked what I had. The still small voice said it thought we had an agreement. I confessed we did and that I was not to count things important and I was not to be a hot shot. I discussed this with my wife and wrote a letter to Paul offering the trade. He responded and said that was the best offer he had ever heard of but India would not allow an American to replace him, and that a Canadian had been chosen to replace him. this was the finish of my understanding of myself and my final handling of the things in my life.

One day, my good friend Merle, who ran the Chrysler dealership across the street in Luray, told me I needed a new car. He said he was going to sell me the Valiant that was parked on the street. "How much?" I asked.

"I'll sell it to you at my cost," he said. "Let's go see how much it is."

I bought that brand-new car for $1,900.

Later, I took care of his wife through a very serious illness—she'd had a very large stroke. I took her to the hospital but things did not improve.

Merle wanted her transferred to Wichita. I sent her to Dr. Leullen, a neurologist. For some reason, he put in a spinal fluid shunt. Suddenly, she woke up and started improving. She came home, and I had the job of managing the shunt and pumping the small balloon under the scalp. It wasn't long before she was back to normal, and it was a delight to see her that way.

My son was large for his age. When he was in the third grade, I discovered he was being a bully. I could not stand to know my son was a bully. I went to the third-grade teacher told her I wouldn't stand for David's being a bully. I said, "I want you to take steps. Go and get him by the shoulder and tell him to stop it. Tell him that his father does not want him to do what he is doing. If you do not do that, I will close my office, come down here, and do it myself. You probably don't want me to do that." As far as I know, that seemed to take care of the problem.

Later, when my children were farther along in school, I asked Mary if David was aggressive or hostile. David's nickname was Hubba. She said she only saw hostility one time. A person was aggravating David, and his reaction was to say, "Either you stop, or you will be a grease spot." That seemed to solve the problem.

My son frequented the local swimming pool. Because he was very large and overweight, a lot of his friends tried to see if they could sink him. He appeared to enjoy every minute of it. He ended up a very good-natured person.

Once when Mary was asked to write an essay, she asked what to do.

She was supposed to write an eight hundred-word theme. "That should be about five or six paragraphs," I said. "What do you want to write?"

"I think I will write about the pilgrims," she answered.

"Go write six paragraphs on the subject," I instructed. "After you do, I will show you how to put them together in an essay and make a beginning and an end." I was taught this method to make an organic whole.

Some time later, I asked her what grade she earned on her essay.

"I got an A-minus," she said.

"Why did you get the minus?"

"I only had 787 words."

"No one counts words," I said. "They just estimate."

She brought me the paper, and written on it was "787 words, A—."

Another time she complained that the students were unruly in an English class, and the teacher was giving volumes of work as punishment.

Another time, she complained that she had pages and pages of work, which was to copy a sentence and underline the subject and predicate.

"Do you know what that is?" I asked. She then correctly identified them in a number of sentences. "Spend fifteen minutes doing that," I said, "and then come to me." She did, and it was done correctly. I then asked, "What were your instructions?"

She said, "To copy."

I said, "Let's go get my copy machine and copy the sentences." We did so, and then she underlined the proper words.

I received a call from school, telling me that Mary had been sent to the office and was crying. I went to the school to talked to the teacher. I asked, "Didn't Mary follow the instructions on your assignment?"

"Yes," the teacher agreed, "but that was sneaky."

"It only proves one thing," I responded, "and that is that I am smarter than you are. I think you will not be working here next year."

"That's because I'm moving," she said.

"The situation really doesn't matter," I told her, "but you might remember my telling you something that could be very valuable: do not make children hate school."

It would have pleased me if my children had followed in my footsteps in a path to God. Contrary to my experiences as a young man, my children had a stormy time at handling their basic motives and desires. Both my children had marriages that ended in divorce. They finally had enough of the crisis to rely on God, asking God to deal with the problems. It appears now that they have straightened out their lives and are having Christ order their lives.

During their time of struggle, I was on my knees, praying and pleading with God for my children. I told him that if they did not serve him, I would be most miserable. I asked him if he really wanted his servant in that much misery. It took a long time, but it appears I've had an answer to my prayers.

I am now close to the end my life. I have had the greatest adventure, and I have been with the love of my life for fifty-eight years. Who could ask for anything more?